Better Health

in Retirement

Keeping well and what to do
if things go wrong

Dr Anne Roberts

© 2001 Anne Roberts

Published by Age Concern England
1268 London Road
London SW16 4ER

First published 2001

Editor Gillian Clarke
Production Vinnette Marshall
Design and typesetting GreenGate Publishing Services, Tonbridge, Kent
Printed and bound in Great Britain by Bell & Bain Ltd, Glasgow

A catalogue record for this book is available from the British Library.

ISBN 0–86242–251–5

Bulk orders
Age Concern England is pleased to offer customised editions of all its titles to UK companies, institutions or other organisations wishing to make a bulk purchase. For further information, please contact the Publishing Department at the address on this page. Tel: 020 8765 7200. Fax: 020 8765 7211. E-mail: books@ace.org.uk.

Contents

About the author

Anne Roberts died while this book was in proof. She was a doctor specialising in the care of older people. Her main interest was in teaching those who look after older people, especially wardens of sheltered housing, staff of residential homes, home care assistants and control centre operators. Her previous books include *A Warden's Guide to Health Care in Sheltered Housing* and *Health Care in Residential Homes* (both Age Concern Books) and *Keeping Well – A guide to health in retirement* (Faber). She developed medication policy and guides to maintaining health throughout the ageing process.

Anne was an almshouse trustee and advised many organisations concerned with health and housing for older people. She leaves two grown-up sons and her husband, a child psychiatrist. She devoted herself professionally to the goal of helping older people to keep their independence and their health.

Acknowledgements

The author thanks everyone who has helped produce this book. In particular, Dr Gerry Bennett, Professor Peter Millard, and Jeremy Fennell, Betty Arrol, Stephen Lowe and Pauline Thompson of Age Concern, for their comments and suggestions.

Introduction

Retirement is a time when we have much more choice about what we do and when. No longer constrained by the need to earn a living, we can become more involved with our hobbies or supporting causes dear to our hearts. Some retired people are so active that they wonder how, before retirement, they found time to fit in their work!

As always, it is important that we look after our health. If possible, we should break bad habits that we've built up over the years – such as smoking or eating unhealthily. In the chapters that follow there are suggestions and guidelines for achieving a healthy lifestyle, including essential body maintenance.

We should never just dismiss aches and pains as 'it's my age' – neither should we let anyone else suggest 'What do you expect, at your age?' Although perhaps we become more susceptible to some illnesses the older we get, many problems have causes that can be put right. Chapter 3 discusses some common illnesses and problems, outlining what they are, why they happen, how the doctor can help and how you can help yourself. It also includes a brief summary of how the National Health System works.

Many older people in the UK will find themselves looking after a spouse or partner, a relative or close friend. (For simplicity, this person is usually referred to as 'your relative'.) Caring for someone is discussed in Chapter 4: The Older Carer.

Whatever your situation, and whatever you want to achieve, good health will make it much more enjoyable. The aim is always 'to die young as late as possible'.

A Healthy Lifestyle

Health in later life depends on a number of factors. First comes heredity, the blueprint handed down by our parents and their ancestors. This is dealt to us like a hand of cards and, unless and until gene therapy becomes widely practised, cannot be altered after the sperm hits the egg. However, just as good card players use their skill to make the most of their cards, a wise and knowledgeable person can adopt a lifestyle that ensures the best outcome despite a family background that contains the usual mix of good and bad. Further, people who know how to reach and use the help of professionals such as doctors, nurses and therapists are well equipped to take charge of the situation if and when they do indeed become ill. This chapter and the section on using services (starting on p 39) contain information designed to help you in these ways.

Eating well

A good diet should contain:

- the right amount of energy (measured in calories or joules) to keep the body within the healthy weight limits for the person's height and build;
- enough nutrients.

Meals should be based on unrefined starchy foods such as potatoes, rice and pasta, with small amounts of protein from lean meat, poultry, fish or lentil foods such as dahl. Add to this dairy products such as milk, cheese and yoghurt, and plenty of fruit and vegetables (nutritionists recommend five portions a day).

People in normal health who can eat and digest the ingredients of a varied diet like this do not need vitamin or mineral supplements. Sometimes, however, these are necessary because of illnesses such as pernicious anaemia (see p 42) or because of the limitations of being housebound; they are then best prescribed by a doctor.

Information about healthy eating is widely available, but the essentials for a retired person are best remembered as 'the six Fs': fibre, fluids, fruit and vegetables, fat, fractures and fun.

Fibre

Older people can counteract their tendency to constipation by increasing the amount of fibre (roughage) in their diets. High-fibre foods include cereals, wholemeal bread, pasta, rice, pulses (such as peas, beans and lentils) and most fruit and vegetables. The quantity should be increased gradually to prevent trouble with wind, and plenty of fluids should be drunk.

Fluids

Many older people become dehydrated because they do not drink enough. This may happen because they fear incontinence or have difficulty in reaching both kitchen and lavatory. The sense of thirst dulls with age, so a dehydrated person may not feel particularly thirsty. Replacing the daily loss of body water in urine, sweat and other body fluids requires 1–2 litres (3–5 pints) a day, and if an adequate amount is taken the urine will be pale, except for first thing in the morning. More fluids will be needed to compensate for extra sweating during hot weather or for watery diarrhoea, vomiting or a discharging ulcer.

Fruit and vegetables

These are the main source of vitamin C, which should be taken daily because it cannot be stored in the body. This vitamin promotes healing of damaged tissues, keeps blood vessels healthy and makes it easier for the body to absorb dietary iron. Vitamin C is destroyed by heat and dissolved by water, so vegetables are best eaten raw or cooked lightly in a little water; microwave cooking or steaming is ideal for vegetables.

Common sense about fat

Everybody needs to eat some fat, to provide the fat-soluble vitamins A, D, E and K. There are two problems connected to an over-high fat intake: obesity and heart disease. Being overweight is unhealthy: diabetes is much more common among older people who are too heavy, as are stroke, coronary heart disease, arthritis, high blood pressure, gallstones, cancer, chest diseases and varicose veins. Fatty foods are very energy-dense, with many calories in small amounts; calories in the form of chocolate, cream and full-fat cheeses are temptingly easy to eat, whereas celery would be much harder work to chew while giving the same amount of energy.

Accumulation of fatty 'fur' called *atheroma* narrows the arteries, and these 'furred pipes' deliver inadequate supplies of blood-borne oxygen to the organs they supply. Angina and other circulation problems result, and complete blockage by a clot formed on the atheromatous wall of an artery can cause a heart attack or stroke. 'Saturated' fats, usually of animal origin, are thought to make this more likely, whereas 'mono-unsaturates' in olive oil and 'poly-unsaturates' in sunflower and corn oil, nuts and oily fish such as herrings and mackerel reduce the risk.

Fractures: eating to prevent them

Bones consist of protein stiffened by calcium, in much the same way as fabric can be stiffened by starch. The underlying protein structure tends to get thinner and weaker with the passing years, especially in women after the menopause. This bone thinning is called *osteoporosis*, and there are various ways of slowing it down (see p 72). Keeping the protein stiff requires an adequate supply of calcium and of vitamin D; this vitamin is needed to get the calcium into the bones. The best sources of calcium are dairy products. Low-fat milk and milk products are a good choice in the diet, because they contain slightly more calcium than whole milk but with fewer calories or risk of atheroma.

Vitamin D is made naturally in our skin on exposure to sunlight. However, not enough may be made in people who do not go out much, especially in more northern countries such as Britain, where our bodies are covered by clothes for most of the year. Vitamin D in food can top up what is made in skin; the best sources are oily fish such as herrings and mackerel.

Fun: eating should be enjoyable!

It is almost always possible to eat a healthy diet and to relish it. Remember that there are no compulsory foods, so find ways of including the essentials in an eating pattern you can enjoy from day to day. The occasional treat – cake, cream tea or fried breakfast – is harmless if not overdone, and makes it easier to eat sensibly the rest of the time.

The essentials: a checklist

Fibre: bread, potatoes and other starches as the basis of every meal.

Fluids: 1–2 litres (3–5 pints) per day, spaced through the day for convenience.

Fruit and vegetables: five portions a day.

Fat: poly- or mono-unsaturates rather than saturates; reduce the total amount if you are trying to lose weight; do not avoid fat altogether.

Fractures: reduce the risk by taking adequate calcium (0.3 litre or ½ pint milk per day; 0.22 kg or ½ lb cheese per week or equivalent in other milk products); one or two portions of oily fish per week for vitamin D.

Fun: what eating should be!

Tips for losing weight

- Set yourself a realistic target by referring to tables of desirable weight for height. Fashion models pictured in magazines are usually unhealthily thin.
- Remember that your metabolic rate (the rate at which your body processes what you eat and drink) slows gradually as the years pass; keeping your figure requires a gentle reduction of calorie intake, particularly the 'empty calories' in sugary or fatty snacks.

- Aim for a slow and steady weight loss of about half a kilo (1 pound) a week.
- Shop when you are not hungry, always make a list beforehand and do not buy on impulse.
- Try to avoid temptation: avoid being near food more than is strictly necessary.
- If you buy edible treats for visiting children, give them the leftovers to take away.
- Keep a stock of fruit and vegetable sticks for nibbling when you are hungry, instead of sugary or fatty snacks such as sweets, crisps, salted nuts or biscuits.
- Avoid calorie-rich drinks, use sweeteners instead of sugar in tea or coffee, and choose low-calorie soft drinks.
- Better still, try to lose a sweet tooth by cutting down gradually on sweet things and re-training your taste buds.
- Check the labels on prepared foods to find out the fat, sugar and calorie content.
- Take smaller portions, and put unfinished dishes out of reach to stop yourself taking second helpings.
- Take more exercise; this will both burn up calories and get you well away from the kitchen.
- Boost your self-esteem by careful dressing and grooming to make the best of your good points.
- You might find joining a weight-watching club useful, to help you keep to the straight and narrow. Do make sure, though, that the organisation you join is reputable and encourages healthy eating and exercise rather than gimmicky reducing fads.

The dangers of smoking

Tobacco is easily the most dangerous drug of addiction in the UK today: it probably contributes to the premature death of about 150,000 people a year. About twenty-five different diseases are more common in smokers; the best known are probably cancers of the lung, mouth and larynx, but smoking is now believed to lessen the body's ability to fight several other cancers, including those of the cervix and bladder. Smokers' blood vessels close up more quickly with the fatty 'fur in the pipes' called *atheroma*, and they are consequently at greater risk of heart attacks, strokes and vascular blockages in the limbs and elsewhere than are non-smokers. Tobacco does not just shorten life, it also reduces its quality; for older people the most important example is the worsening of the coughs and bronchitis, which can make the winter a misery.

Many older people took up smoking when its dangers were less well known; this was particularly so in World War 2, when cigarettes were easily and cheaply available in the armed services. In addition, the present danger of tonight's blitz or tomorrow's possible invasion seemed much more real than a shadowy future. Nicotine is very addictive; once 'hooked', the smoker can have uncomfortable withdrawal symptoms. Another cigarette can relieve these temporarily, and a vicious circle of smoking–withdrawal–smoking–withdrawal is set up.

The news for people trying to quit is not all bad, however. Many find giving up easier than they expected, and the worst withdrawal symptoms are generally over in a month. Weight gain is usually slight, if it occurs at all, and it would take an increase of 63.5 kg (10 stone) to be as dangerous as 20 cigarettes a day. It is never too late to give up: the risks of heart and blood vessel diseases fall from the time the last cigarette is stubbed out, and after ten years' abstinence the chances of lung cancer approach those of a non-smoker. Even people who are over 80 years old when they give up feel the benefits of a clearer chest, easier breathing and a quicker recovery from winter coughs and colds. Contact Quitline (details on p 140) for information and help with trying to stop smoking.

If your previous attempts to stop smoking have been frustrated by irritability and cravings for a cigarette, you might consider using a replacement source of nicotine to help reduce these symptoms. This is nicotine replacement therapy, or NRT. There are five forms:

- chewing gum;
- skin patches;
- an inhaler;
- a nasal spray;
- tablets that you place under your tongue.

They are most useful in heavier smokers (20 or more cigarettes a day). Unfortunately, nicotine replacement therapy is not generally available on NHS prescription but you can obtain it over the counter in the chemist's shop. Discuss with the pharmacist or your doctor whether these preparations might help you.

How to become a non-smoker

- Think out some reasons for quitting that matter to you: you may have a spouse with chest problems or a new grandchild who would benefit from smoke-free air.
- Get your family and friends to support and encourage your efforts; perhaps someone else could give up, too, and you could support each other.
- Spot the circumstances when temptation is likely, and take avoiding action. For instance, get up from the table after a meal and do something to distract you from the thought of the after-dinner cigarette.
- Try to avoid other smokers.
- Do not have cigarettes in the house, and put ashtrays and lighters away out of sight.
- Give your mouth something else to do: chew sugarless gum or crunch carrot sticks; even cleaning your teeth may get you over a bad moment.
- Put aside the money you save for something you want, but spend a little of it on a 'prize' for kicking the habit.

Enjoying alcohol in later life

What is sensible drinking?

Most people who enjoy alcohol use it sensibly, and there is some evidence that light drinking can reduce the chances of heart disease. A minority of people drink to excess, with serious consequences for their physical and mental health and happiness. On the whole, older people drink less than their juniors; however, ageing changes in the body mean that older people are especially vulnerable to the ill effects of excess alcohol. This is especially so for women, whose bodies contain less of the muscular and organ tissues that break down alcohol and eliminate it from the body.

How much is too much?

The risks of light drinking are very small, but the dangers get progressively greater as more is drunk. A sensible limit for older drinkers is:

- 3–4 units two or three times a week (total 6–12 units) for an older man;
- 2–3 units two or three times a week (total 4–9 units) for an older woman.

The total amount should be spaced through the week, with some alcohol-free days (AFDs).

A 'unit' is a single measure of spirits, or half a pint of normal-strength beer or a pub measure of wine, sherry, port or vermouth. Low-alcohol drinks vary in their strength from very weak to about a third the strength of ordinary drinks, so it makes sense to check the Alcohol By Volume (ABV) figures on the label. Remember that there are extra units in strong beers, large glasses and drinks poured at home with a generous hand!

Too much of a good thing

People of any age who drink to excess run extra health risks: these include liver damage, bleeding from the stomach lining, painful legs from nerve damage, high blood pressure, vitamin deficiency, sexual impotence and depressive illness sometimes ending in suicide. Older people may develop these, but they are also more likely to suffer from mental problems; acute confusion can follow a drinking bout or withdrawal from heavy drinking, while long-term alcohol abuse causes brain damage from a direct poisonous effect and also from the poor eating habits and frequent head injuries that often go with it. Other hazards include a tendency to fall and an increased risk of incontinence, both because of the increased need to pass urine and the decreased awareness, mobility and dexterity in dealing with this. Poor eating habits make things worse, and drunken behaviour leads to social isolation. Alcohol abuse may shorten life and, contrary to bar-room gossip, it rarely results in a merry one.

Developing safer habits

Most of us who enjoy social drinking do not run these risks, but a little thought about our personal drinking pattern may be useful. Here is a checklist of useful tactics:

- Find out how much alcohol you really drink: keep a drinking diary for a week.
- Note the places, people and circumstances that go with drinking; if you need to cut down a bit, avoid temptation.
- Find a non-alcoholic drink you enjoy and alternate it with your preferred alcoholic drink.
- Work out your limit before the occasion, and give yourself a small 'reward' if you manage to stick to it.
- When entertaining, make it easy for guests to drink sparingly or avoid alcohol altogether. Have a good supply of non-alcoholic drinks and offer them frequently.
- If you (or someone you know) have a drink problem that is too much for you, consider seeking help from your doctor or nurse. Alternatively, you could contact Alcohol Concern for advice and help (for the address, see p 131).

Keeping active

Many of us have bad memories of humiliation and failure in games lessons at school, and feel relief at having left these behind us. However, it is a mistake to let such experiences put us off being active and vigorous in retirement. The main advantage of fitness in later life is that it enables us to do want we want to, easily and unaided, which gives us a liberating control over our own lives. It also helps to prevent many common illnesses: angina, heart attacks and strokes, high blood pressure, diabetes, obesity, osteoporosis, chronic fatigue and depression are all more common in the unfit. Exercise also increases stamina of the heart and lungs, strengthens muscles and bones, and improves balance and the suppleness of joints. Even people in their 90s can benefit from increased activity, and useful and enjoyable exercises can be performed while sitting in a chair. 'Use it and keep it' is an important maxim, especially for older people.

What sort of exercise?

Although older people can and do run marathons, no one advises sedentary people over 60 to leap straight from their armchairs to the running track; this may lead to injury and even less activity. However, the risks of exercise can be over-emphasised, and far more older people are limited by doing too little than hurt themselves by over-enthusiasm. It is almost always possible to find a suitable way to improve the physical fitness of even the frailest older person.

Good ways to keep active

- Walking is cheap, and requires no special equipment. Try to walk 1–2 miles a day, at a speed that accelerates the heart beat and warms the body. Aim to work up to a speed of 3 miles an hour if possible.
- Cycling is good for the body and for the environment, but check that road conditions around you are not too dangerous. It is sensible for cyclists to wear a helmet and reflective clothing, and to keep their machines well maintained; lights and brakes are particularly important.
- Swimming is especially suitable for people with arthritis, as the water takes some of the body's weight. It strengthens the supporting muscles of the back, improves spinal mobility and relieves back pain. Some swimming pools have sessions when only older people can use them, and you may want to check on this.
- Exercise classes provide an opportunity to keep fit with expert supervision and in congenial company. Your local authority's adult education department may provide these, or you may want to contact Exercise England (formerly the Exercise Association of England) or the Extend organisation, which specialise in work with older people or those with disabilities.
- Dancing and yoga classes may be another way to keep fit and have fun at your own pace.
- You may want to keep up a previous sporting interest, in tennis or golf, for instance. However, it is unwise to try to compete with younger people, or with rosy memories of one's prowess long ago!

Sensible precautions for fitness

If you are fit and healthy, you probably don't need to get your doctor's advice before beginning an exercise programme. Nevertheless, if you are in any doubt, it might be worth checking first. The following are some sensible precautions to take.

- If you are having regular treatment for high blood pressure or for chest, heart or joint disease, it is wise to ask your doctor's advice before starting an exercise programme.
- Always start an exercise session with a gentle 'warm up', increase activity slowly and 'cool down' at the end. Wait until two hours after eating before you start, and have a glass of water every half hour.
- Pay attention to your body: you should not feel giddy or exhausted while exercising. If you do, slow down or if necessary stop. No exercise should hurt at the time: do not force a joint to do more than it comfortably can.
- Stop and rest if you become unduly short of breath, feel sick or develop chest pains or palpitations (an uncomfortable awareness of the heartbeat); if these do not get better quickly, see the doctor.
- Do not exercise when unwell, especially when you have a temperature. Avoid exercising outdoors when it is very cold, and take it easy when the weather is warm and humid.

Having noted all these warnings, be aware that far more older people suffer from the effects of inactivity than are ever hurt by taking exercise!

Looking after yourself

Safe as houses?

Preventing accidents at home requires a balance of adventurousness and caution. Older people should take only interesting and enjoyable risks; the benefits of keeping a cat may be worth the small risk of falling over it, but a torn carpet does no one any good and may catch an unwary foot. It is possible to maintain independence without being reckless by avoiding some of the common causes of falls; no one, young or old, should climb on furniture to reach high objects, rather than fetching a safe stepladder designed for the purpose.

Re-positioning power points a metre from the floor and re-siting cupboards may reduce the need to bend or stretch into unstable postures. It can also help to fit equipment such as grab rails in bathrooms or lavatories, or to change from a bath to a shower with level access and a seat. You can get advice about aids and adaptations from an occupational therapist through the social services department, but there are sometimes long delays. In this case you may consider buying what you need through a chain chemist/pharmacist or a Disabled Living Centre. Aids to home nursing during illness can often be borrowed from the Red Cross.

There are special dangers for older people in tipping the head back to look sharply upwards, and in rising too quickly from a lying or sitting position: both of these can lead to unsteadiness and a nasty fall. Giddy spells can often frighten people into immobility; they should instead see their GP and ask for investigation and treatment to eliminate the cause if possible.

Fire precautions

The most dangerous object in the kitchen is the chip pan; changing to oven chips makes sense for both safety and good nutrition. A fire blanket is especially useful to smother flames from a burning pan.

All open fires should be guarded, and electric heaters with exposed elements replaced. Clothing should be non-inflammable, and pyjamas may be safer than floating night-dresses. Smoke alarms may be especially useful for awakening sleepers to danger at night. It is very dangerous for older people to smoke in bed or when drowsing in an armchair, as upholstery and bedding may be set alight and emit poisonous fumes. The safest tactic is, of course, to give up smoking altogether.

Keeping warm

Our perception of body temperature becomes blunted as the years pass, so even the most sensible and intelligent older person may be unaware that they are becoming dangerously cold. It is sensible to fit room thermometers and maintain living room and bedroom temperatures above 20 degrees Celsius (68 degrees Fahrenheit).

Some people like to live and sleep in a single room during very cold weather, and so save on heating costs. Make sure that you are claiming all your benefit entitlements; you may like to refer to Age Concern's annual publication *Your Rights* for further information (see p 148). A factsheet called *Help with heating* (Factsheet 1) is available from Age Concern's Information Line. It gives details of grants available to householders over 60 to make their homes more energy efficient, for instance by insulation and draught proofing. It also gives useful advice on payment schemes and how to prevent the risk of having the gas and electricity disconnected. Details of how to get a range of factsheets are given on page 149.

Averting the threat of crime

Some older people worry so much about falling victim to a criminal that they restrict their activities and spoil their enjoyment of life. Below are a few suggestions for more sensible precautions; these should make your mind easier without interfering too much with your outings and pleasures.

- Ask the Crime Prevention Officer (CPO) from the local police station to check your home security and advise on any further measures that should be taken.
- Be careful to lock the doors and windows every time you go out; a note to yourself on the inside of the front door may be a useful reminder.
- Keep only small, necessary amounts of cash in the house; keep savings in a bank, building society or post office.
- Fit a spy-hole and security chain to your door; do not remove the chain until you have identified your visitor.
- Insist on seeing evidence of identity before admitting meter readers, maintenance staff or repair people.
- Join your local Neighbourhood Watch Scheme, or consider starting one; your local police station will be able to advise about this.
- On the street, avoid lonely or badly lit areas, especially at night; the CPO will know where is and is not safe.
- When you go out, take only the cash you need, and keep valuable jewellery out of sight, perhaps under a scarf, cuff or glove.
- Keep your door keys or car keys ready in your pocket so that you can use them quickly if you become nervous.

- Ask a neighbour to keep an eye on your house if you go away, and to check for tell-tale piles of mail or free newspapers.
- Further suggestions about safety can be found in Age Concern's Factsheet 33 *Crime prevention for older people.*

Sex in later life

Our relationships are an important part of our lives whatever age we are. Even in this frank age, it still sometimes surprises and even shocks younger people that their elders are sexually interested and active. Older people have known this all along, though they may be reticent about this private aspect of their lives.

There is of course nothing 'dirty' or 'unnatural' about physical love in later life, whether it is between people of the same or the opposite sex. Normal ageing changes, whether social, psychological or physical, affect performance less than is sometimes thought. Sex life can even improve in old age, when many years of tenderness and companionship are expressed within it, and bedtime after early-morning tea or after lunch is more useful for a cuddle than a weary late evening. A man's erections tend to become less firm with increasing age, but are often still sufficient for intercourse to be satisfactory for both parties. A woman's response becomes slower both physically and psychologically after the menopause, but the capacity to enjoy sexual love is not lost. If 'technical problems' develop, it is usually possible either to correct them or to find other ways of expressing love and relieving sexual tension.

Loss of a sexual partner by death is of course very common in later life. There are many more women left in this position than men, as men in general die younger and tend to marry or form new partnerships with women younger than themselves. Bereaved older people often complain that no one wants to listen to their accounts of how much they miss the sexual part of their relationship. Older bereaved gay people suffer particularly from a lack of the kindness and support that widows or widowers can usually expect. The Lesbian and Gay Bereavement Project (see p 138) may be able to help here.

Sexual problems

Impotence, sometimes called erectile dysfunction, is the inability to have firm enough erections for intercourse. There are a number of different causes; some of these are psychological, such as depressive illness, anxiety or the fear of 'failure', especially when this has already happened once or more. Physical factors can also play a part; some prescribed medicines interfere with erections, but can often be replaced by others that do the same job without affecting sexual function. Impotence can occur in illnesses such as diabetes which damage the nerves to the penis, and in nervous system diseases such as multiple sclerosis, or stroke. Having an erection depends on there being a good blood supply to the penis; if the man's arteries are partially blocked with atheroma, the blood supply may be insufficient for the penis to become fully erect. In addition, lifestyle factors can be important: alcohol and drug abuse and heavy smoking are all believed to contribute to the problem.

There are several possible approaches to potency problems. One option is for the man to consult his GP with a view to finding out what has gone wrong and putting it right. Many cases have a psychological basis; in some the man will be so anxious to 'perform' well that his feelings will interfere with his erection. In others the sexual problem can be a sign that the underlying personal relationship is troubled. Some GPs will feel able to deal with these problems, while others will want to pass on at least some cases to a specialist in psychosexual counselling or an organisation such as Relate (for the address, see p 142).

Sometimes there will be a physical cause of impotence, which the GP will diagnose in the usual way before giving appropriate advice. In other cases he or she may suspect that a prescribed medicine is the culprit, and may make a change in the patient's drug therapy that will put things right.

In more unusual or difficult cases the GP may want to refer the person to a hospital specialist for further investigation and treatment. Sometimes it will be possible to eliminate the cause of the trouble, while in others it may be best to produce an erection by some other means. At the simplest level, a device is available that makes the penis swell by creating a vacuum around it, after which an elastic band is positioned round the base of the penis to preserve the erection until intercourse has taken place. Another useful option is an injection into the penis which the man learns to give himself. Yet another is transurethral therapy, when a small quantity of drug is inserted up the urethra (the bladder's drainage tube) and absorbed, giving an erection. A new treatment is the drug sildenafil, sold as Viagra. It is taken by mouth an hour before sexual activity is planned, after which it will produce an erection in response to sexual stimulation. A drawback is that it interacts with a group of drugs called nitrates, commonly taken by people with heart disease, so people with erectile dysfunction and heart disease must use another method. (At the time of writing, Viagra on NHS prescription is only available to men with certain conditions, such as diabetes, Parkinson's disease or prostate cancer.)

Very occasionally, surgical treatment is used. One technique aims to give the man a permanent small erection by implanting silicon rods into the penis. Another method involves inserting a device that can be inflated to stiffen the penis when a bulb in the scrotum is squeezed. Such procedures may correct the purely mechanical problem, but will leave untouched any psychological aspects of the difficulty. In addition, such treatment may not be available free on the NHS, and private insurance schemes will not always cover its costs, so prospective patients should discuss the whole issue with their GP first. It is also wise to be wary of 'cures' advertised in newspapers and magazines, as some substances sold as 'aphrodisiacs' may have harmful effects.

Another approach concentrates on using other techniques apart from penetration for expressing physical love and relieving sexual tension. Kissing, cuddling and stimulation of breasts, clitoris and penis with the hand or mouth of a loving partner can give as much pleasure and as satisfying an orgasm as sexual intercourse with penis in vagina. Of course, many older people either know this already or can work it out for themselves. However, some may have been brought up to regard such activities as abnormal and in some way blameworthy. Such people may be helped by an assurance from someone whose opinion they respect that any form of sexual expression that two adults both enjoy and which hurts neither is 'allowed'; such 'permission-giving' can be very liberating to a loving relationship.

Women after the menopause

When the production of female hormones starts to diminish at this point in a woman's life, the process of sexual excitement that prepares the body for intercourse becomes slower. The lining of the vagina becomes less elastic, and lubrication of the tissues takes longer and may be less efficient. Consequently, some women may find intercourse painful and prefer to avoid it, while loving partners can be reluctant to make an approach that may hurt the person they are fond of. Although the resulting loss of sexual pleasure is sad, it is even sadder if a combination of sexual frustration and half-unconscious resentment undermines a long-standing relationship, but this can easily happen.

Fortunately, this state of affairs can usually be put right. A simple water-based lubricant such as K-Y Jelly, Replens or Senselle may be enough to make sex pain-free and pleasurable again. All these preparations can be bought without a prescription. Other women may benefit from the replacement of their lost hormones, either as a hormone cream or pessary to be applied to the vagina or as standard hormone replacement therapy (HRT) by tablet, patch or implant.

The first person to go to for help should be your GP. It is perfectly proper to ask to see a doctor of the same sex if this would make you feel more comfortable. Most practices now include doctors of both sexes, but if not a nurse may be a useful go-between. Some GPs are very knowledgeable about these matters, and helpful in their treatment, but where this is not the case you may want to ask for a specialist referral to a urologist, gynaecologist or menopause clinic. Another good source of advice is the family planning or well woman clinic; even an older woman who is self-conscious when visiting such a clinic may feel able to make a telephone enquiry.

Disability and sexual difficulties

Some people with disabilities find that their sexual function is affected, and this can come about in a number of ways. Direct damage to the brain, spinal cord or the nerves that supply the sexual organs may interfere with their function; this may occur with stroke, in Parkinson's disease, or from accidents, tumours or operations that destroy nerve tissue. Women may give up sex after a hysterectomy, though this seems more often to have psychological causes than physical ones. The open (retropubic) prostatectomy operation that leaves a scar on the man's abdomen can render him impotent, but this can also be due to the disease (especially prostate cancer) that made the operation necessary. The nerve damage cannot be put right, but affected men benefit from careful explanation of the likely effects before the operation, the chance to mourn their lost potency afterwards and specific advice about other ways of expressing their sexuality. The 'transurethral' prostatectomy that is done with slender instruments slid up the penis does not affect potency but may cause 'retrograde ejaculation'. In this condition the semen released at orgasm rushes upwards into the bladder, rather than gushing out of the end of the penis in the usual way. Although this feels different to both partners, it often does not affect either person's enjoyment, especially if the subject is discussed before the operation. Only the small minority of men with retrograde ejaculation who wish to father more children need special help to enable them to do so. Among organisations that may help people with sexual difficulties are SPOD (Sexual and Personal Relationships of People with a Disability), the Impotence Association and the British Association for Sexual and Marital Therapy (contact details in the 'Useful addresses' section at the back of this book).

Essential body maintenance

Regular checks on eyes, teeth and feet keep them functioning well. If anything is wrong, it can be identified and treated early, and the best results can be obtained.

Eyes

The only 'normal' ageing change in the eye likely to be noticed by its owner is a loss of focusing power of the lens. This makes it more difficult to read small print, but the difficulty can be corrected by reading glasses. Other changes are not normal, and should be discussed with a doctor. Some mean that sight is under threat, and the problem should be reported to a doctor or eye hospital *at once*. These are:

- sudden loss of vision, even if it returns on its own;
- disturbance of the 'field of vision' – black patches, or an effect like a black curtain or shutter covering part of what you are looking at;
- seeing flashing lights, or the appearance of coloured haloes round lamps;
- pain and redness of the eye.

Older people whose eyes are giving no trouble should have an eye examination at least every two years. This is because serious conditions such as glaucoma can cause considerable eye damage without producing obvious symptoms; it can, however, be picked up on an eye test. Eye examinations are now free for both men and women over the age of 60.

Good lighting makes the most of sight. It is particularly useful to have a good reading light (60 watts) in a flexible holder directed over the shoulder.

Teeth

People with bad teeth can sometimes eat only soft foods, and the poor diet that results can affect their general health. Uneven and discoloured permanent teeth spoil the appearance, as may the 'gummy' mouth of someone whose ill-fitting and painful dentures are left unworn. It makes good sense for older people as well as younger ones to go to the dentist regularly. People with their own teeth should have a check-up every six months, while those with full dentures should visit the dentist once a year. Apart from checking that the dentures fit and making adjustments if necessary, this gives the dentist a chance to ensure that the mouth is generally healthy, and in particular to make sure that there are no signs of cancer. This usually appears as a mouth ulcer that does not heal in a fortnight. It is curable if caught early enough, so a mouth ulcer like this should be shown to a dentist without delay.

Once registered with a dentist for NHS treatment, you are entitled to all the care and treatment needed to make your mouth healthy. If you are not registered with a dentist, friends or your GP may be able to suggest one. You can also look at a list of NHS dentists at the offices of the health authority, at main post offices and at the public library. Very frail or disabled people may be treated at home by the Community Dental Service.

The local health authority or the community health council will tell you how to get in touch with this service. It is important to re-register with your NHS dentist every 15 months; if you don't do so, you may lose your entitlement to continuing care with that dentist.

NHS dental treatment is not free to all older people, though certain people on low incomes may be exempt from charges. Cosmetic treatment and other measures that are not strictly necessary to dental health need to be paid for out of the person's own pocket, and private fees can be much higher than NHS ones. Up-to-date information on the charging procedure can be found in Age Concern's Factsheet 5 *Dental care in retirement*.

Feet

Feet sometimes spread as the years pass, so your size may change in width or length or both. It is worth taking the trouble to find well-fitting shoes, though this is not always easy. If you have difficulty finding a supplier, you could ask a chiropodist or at a Disabled Living Centre, or write to the Society of Shoe Fitters (see p 143).

If your eyesight or joint mobility have deteriorated a little as the years have passed, you may have difficulty in cutting your toenails. There are nail-cutting services in some areas; social services or your local Age Concern group/organisation will be able to tell you about this.

Regular application of E45 cream, available from the chemist, can help to ward off corns, calluses and hard skin. If they do develop, however, it is better not to tackle them yourself, but to see a chiropodist. This is because older feet tend to have a poor blood supply and heal less well if they are injured.

NHS chiropody is free to people over 65 years old, but waiting lists are often long. If you need to find a private chiropodist, look for the letters SRCh (State Registered Chiropodist) after his or her name. Regular chiropody at least every six months is essential for people with diabetes. This is because changes in the blood vessels of people with diabetes mean that injuries heal poorly. Also, nerve damage tends to reduce the foot's sensitivity to pain, so infected wounds that should hurt but do not may be unwittingly neglected. There will often be an experienced chiropodist in attendance at the diabetic clinic.

Sense about health checks

'Screening' for a condition involves looking for a disease in someone who has no obvious signs of it yet. It is only useful when:

- There is an easy, safe test for the condition. (It is easy, for instance, to take a smear of the surface cells of the cervix, while it would be neither safe nor easy to take a sample of brain tissue.)
- People are willing to use the testing procedure. (Though testing stool samples for blood is a useful way of detecting bowel cancer at a treatable stage, there is great unwillingness to collect the stool sample.)
- The condition is treatable once detected, and the earlier it is diagnosed the better will be the outlook for the patient.

Although there are obvious benefits of screening, there are also costs, both in money and in emotional distress. Some testing procedures are unpleasant or uncomfortable, and may discourage people from attending again. A 'false positive' result can cause a great deal of needless distress before it can be shown to be a mistake; 1 in 10 women who have a mammogram are recalled for further testing, while only 1 in 200 prove to have breast cancer. On the other hand, a negative result can give a false sense of security, and prevent the person concerned from taking much-needed steps to improve health, such as stopping smoking. Tests also use resources and cost money that might have been better used elsewhere.

Taking all these costs and benefits into account, there are three tests for women that are probably worth the trouble and expense. One of these is also useful to men.

Mammography This is a type of X-ray that can detect breast cancer at an early and treatable stage, before it can be felt by an examining hand. Mammography by the NHS starts at the age of 50 and at the moment is repeated every three years until the age of 65. There is no medical reason for stopping testing after 65, as breast cancer continues to be common in older women. Women of 65 and over who wish to continue having mammograms should ask for this to be done.

A cervical smear This should be taken every three years from the start of sexual activity until the age of 65, or until the clinic advises that further ones are unnecessary; this may happen any time from the age of 55 onwards. There are several reasons for this. First, tests show that a woman aged 55 or over with a series of normal smears behind her is very unlikely to develop cervical cancer during the rest of her life. Secondly, most cervical cancers in older women are found in those who never had a smear at all. Thirdly, it becomes progressively more difficult and painful to get a good smear from an older woman.

Blood pressure measurement This is important for men and women. Blood pressure is the force that keeps the blood circulating round the body. Higher than usual blood pressure is not a disease in itself, but it increases the risk of illnesses such as stroke or heart attack. Blood pressure should be checked every year; this is especially important for people of Afro-Caribbean descent, who are more likely to have high blood pressure and are especially prone to strokes. (The reason for this is not known.) If you have not had your blood pressure measured recently, ask for this to be done by your GP or practice nurse.

Other tests These are not offered routinely, but may be done if a person's special circumstances suggest that they might be useful. For instance, blood lipids such as the different types of cholesterol might be measured in a family whose members tend to develop heart disease rather early in life, but this test would not be necessary for everyone.

When to see the doctor

It is sensible to see the doctor whenever a health problem is starting to interfere with your life – if, for instance, poor bladder control is making you unwilling to go out, or poor hearing is interfering with your social life.

There are also some symptoms that should be discussed with the doctor as soon as they appear. In almost all cases an innocent explanation is found, but very occasionally they prove to be due to a serious illness such as cancer. The sooner this is diagnosed, the better the results of treatment will be. See the doctor as soon as you can if you notice:

- a lump in the breast;
- an ulcer that takes more that two weeks to heal on your skin or in your mouth;

- bleeding from the back passage, blood streaks in spit or a blood-stained discharge from the vagina;
- hoarseness persisting for more than three weeks;
- a persistent cough, especially if you are a smoker;
- stroke signs (see p 76) that come on in minutes and rapidly get better; this is called a transient ischaemic attack or TIA;
- severe impairment or complete loss of sight, or of part of the field of vision. People with giant cell arteritis (see p 60) often have severe headaches and tenderness of the face and scalp, too.

People of any age have a right to chose their own lifestyle. However, there is now evidence that cultivating healthy living habits can increase well-being in later years, adding to the enjoyable lifetime, rather than just dragging out dependency. The aim is always 'to die young as late as possible'.

Health for Mind and Spirit

Some older people try to spend their retirement filling out the gaps in their lives to make a meaningful whole. This is always a very personal process, and there are no quick and sure-fire ways to peace and fulfilment. However, some strategies seem to work again and again in helping towards a happy and rewarding retirement. A few of these are described below.

Keeping mentally active

Learning

The older mind needs exercise to keep it functioning at optimum level. Fortunately, provided physical health is retained, there is little evidence that mental ability declines significantly until extreme old age. True, it takes longer to learn new material by rote as the years pass; this may slow the process of learning a new language, for instance, compared with young adults. However, this may be offset by the benefits of retained long-term learning; a previously studied language may have roots and structure similar to those of the new one. It seems that older learners do best at a topic that interests them and that they are motivated to study. They also need to be allowed to go at their own pace, and to have a supportive tutor to tide them over any difficulties. Given this sort of learning environment, many older people surprise themselves by the pleasure and satisfaction they get improving on their early education, going more deeply into a topic that has long interested them, coming to terms with modern technology or just broadening their mental horizons.

Educational resources

Below are some suggestions to help you with your studies.

Your local library Resources and staff may be available to help you with personal study or research. Newspapers, periodicals, records and tapes will be available as well as books, and you should have the use of a photocopier. Some libraries provide help in learning to use computers, and it may be possible to access the Internet. The library is also a very important source of information about education services provided by the local authority, and about local interest groups; these cover topics such as local history and may also study the lives and works of local authors and other notables. Archives and other historical material are often stored in libraries, and may be studied by interested people.

Your local authority education office This is responsible for providing adult education classes in the daytime and the evening, usually with concessionary rates for pensioners, though you may have to ask for these. Sadly, some classes have been closed because of shortage of money.

Your local school Some schools welcome older people who are willing to share their memories as oral history. In others, older people join the younger students in preparing and sitting for public exams such as GCSE and A level.

Age Concern England has several sources of help; the Information and Policy Division can provide information and publishes a newsletter about educational and leisure opportunities; Age Resource (based at Age Concern) aims to help with volunteering and campaigning as well as education, while Ageing Well promotes positive health in retirement (see p 145 for Age Concern's contact information).

Open University This offers a wide range of long and short courses and study packs. Those covering topics such as retirement, social welfare, caring for older people and mental health in old age may be especially interesting to older students (see p 140 for contact information).

University of the Third Age (U3A) This is a network of local groups of older people who learn together in self-help groups by pooling their knowledge and experience. The national office (see p 144) has details of local branches, publishes *Third Age News* and has resources to start up and support new branches.

Volunteering

Older people may well feel that they have experience and skills that they are able to share when, in retirement, they have time on their hands. You can find details of opportunities nearby from your local Council for Voluntary Service, Citizens Advice Bureau or the library. Perhaps you would like to help adults with literacy needs or children with reading; try asking at the education office or your local school. Churches, charity shops and political parties also need volunteers. The two organisations listed below are further sources of information:

- REACH finds part-time, expenses-only jobs for retired people who want to give charities the benefit of their business and professional experience (for their address, see p 141).
- Age Resource, based at Age Concern England, also aims to promote the recognition of older people's life skills in voluntary work over a wide range of areas, including caring and the environment.

Stress and how to cope with it

Stress is part of life, before or after retirement. It is not always bad: before a demanding task, such as making a speech, the stress of the situation is what tones up the body and mind to extra effort and improved performance. People with too little stress in their lives – no change or challenge – may set tasks for themselves, or add a little spice of danger with anything from a fun-fair ride to a parachute jump (not recommended for the over-50s!).

However, too much of the wrong sort of stress is definitely unhealthy, though only the person concerned can know how much is too much. Big life events, such as moving house, are more upsetting than little ones, and the stress is aggravated if the change is unexpected – for instance, due to illness – and is unfamiliar, as for someone who has stayed put most of their lives.

The physical reactions of the body to stress are a proper part of the 'flight or fight' reaction that served Stone Age man well in dealing with sabre-toothed tigers. In the modern world they are mainly unhelpful, uncomfortable and may be wrongly interpreted as symptoms of an illness. Common ones include palpitations, tense painful muscles (especially of the head and shoulders), a sick feeling, diarrhoea, sweating, backache, a dry mouth and throat, chest discomfort, headaches, change in appetite and difficulty in sleeping.

Mental changes also occur: the person feels pressured but finds it difficult to relax, and may make things worse by trying ever harder. People who have difficulty in balancing conflicting responsibilities may become frustrated and aggressive. Poor concentration and indecisiveness make tasks ever more difficult, so stressed people become fussy, irritable and hard to please. They are unable to relax and enjoy things even when the pressures on them ease. Friends and family may find them clingy, wanting constant reassurance, or withdrawn and indifferent; they may be extra difficult to help if they deny their obvious distress and refuse help from any quarter.

If all this sounds uncomfortably familiar to you or those around you, it may be time to take stock and list the causes of stress in your life. The next step is to divide the causes into potentially changeable factors, circumstances that will improve with time and things that can't be changed; these groups are to be tackled in different ways.

While working on the changeable factors, it will help to have a confidant, someone you can discuss things with openly and honestly without the need to impress them with your coping abilities or demonstrate your 'niceness'. If you are fortunate, there may be someone in the circle of your family and friends whom you trust in this way and who trusts you in return. Then settle down to think about and discuss your wants and needs; consider the likely impact on others where conflict arises, but remember that you are a person of worth and you are entitled to put yourself first some of the time. Self-sacrifice can be an aggressive act, leading to an atmosphere of resentment and depression, and standing up for yourself is sometimes both appropriate and kind.

If appropriate, consider looking for professional help. Consult your GP for worries about illness, or get in touch with the social services if practical help would be useful. You might for instance be a carer and need some time to yourself, while your relative has some respite care. Perhaps advice or help from a voluntary agency might meet the case: Relate for relationship difficulties, for instance, or the Samaritans (08457 90 90 90) if you are desperate for a kindly listening ear. Lists of voluntary agencies and self-help groups are available in libraries.

Some difficulties are unchangeable, or will be solved only by the passage of time. People sometimes feel obscurely guilty about their misfortunes, and blame themselves for being less capable than the people around them. It can help to remember that people's public faces all conceal a share of bruises from hard knocks; no one is immune to problems. Again, a confidant can help you to vent your feelings. It may be tempting to withdraw into yourself, but try to resist this impulse. There are benefits to looking outwards, building a circle of friends and acquaintances, and occupying yourself with other activities; those involving music or physical exercise seem particularly helpful in preventing brooding and promoting sleep. Look after your physical health by eating properly and having adequate rest. Do not add to your problems by seeking solace in alcohol, tobacco or drugs; they always turn out to be false friends.

Relaxation techniques

These can help reduce stress and promote sleep if you are feeling tense. There are many books and audiotapes on this topic, but the essentials are described below.

1 *Controlled breathing* Put your hands on your abdomen and take slow, regular breaths in and out; feel your abdomen lift and fall under your hands as you do this. Some people count as they breathe in and out, while others prefer to recite a prayer or mantra in their heads.
2 *Loosening the muscles* Begin by clenching your fists and tightening all your muscles for a count of three. Then let go, from your toes upwards, relaxing all the tension and letting the muscles go loose. Note how this feels, and try to relax even further, again upwards from the feet.

3 *Imaging* When you have relaxed and steadied your breathing, call up a restful picture in your mind – perhaps of peaceful scenery or a favourite activity.

These exercises require a little practice, and are best done once or twice a day until they become familiar. Once learned, they are a useful resource whenever you are under pressure.

Tips for long-term stress reduction

- Sort out your true priorities.
- Plan ahead.
- Share your anxieties, rather than dwelling on them alone.
- Take care of your physical health.
- Don't be too hard on yourself.
- Don't be too proud to ask for help.

Sleep

We all tend to need less sleep as the years pass, and to sleep less deeply. Older people often seem to under-estimate their amount of sleep; someone who has surfaced sufficiently to look at the clock on several occasions may well believe they 'never slept a wink' when in fact they had a reasonable night. Again, a short night may be added to by a series of naps after lunch and in front of evening television, until quite a respectable total is reached. Left to itself, a healthy body and mind of any age gets the sleep it needs, compensating on succeeding nights for any short-term losses without affecting health in any way.

How to help yourself to better sleep

- Try to establish a pattern to late evening; go to bed as near as possible at the same time, and wind down your activities beforehand; a hot bath may aid relaxation.
- Ask yourself whether there is a health problem that is preventing you from sleeping. Prostate problems, coughs, pain from any cause and depressive illness all interfere with sleep; if you suffer from any of these, see the doctor.

- Avoid stimulants such as tea and coffee after about 6pm, or use decaffeinated varieties. Some people find that a milky drink helps them to settle, and you may want to try this. Do not, of course, drink large quantities of any fluid immediately before bedtime, because this will increase your need to go to the lavatory during the night. However, if you are over 50, you should be prepared to get up once; restricting fluids to avoid this may lead to dehydration.

- Remember that alcohol used as a sedative is both inefficient and dangerous. Though the modest nightcap taken by many older people is harmless, taking enough to become fuddled and sleepy works for a short while but is followed by a period of 'rebound' wakefulness in the small hours. The temptation then is to repeat and increase the dose, with all the risks of confusion, unsteadiness and dependence.

- Do not take naps in the daytime, and try to take enough exercise in the fresh air to induce a pleasant tiredness.

- Treat sleeping tablets as a short-term last resort, to help re-establish a disordered sleep pattern or to tide you over a bad time, such as an illness. Co-operate with your doctor if she or he wants to stop the tablets you have taken for some time; you may have poorer sleep for a few nights while your body gets used to doing without them, but you will soon re-establish a new sleep pattern, perhaps with the help of the steps described above.

Loss and bereavement

Older people say that the worst thing about ageing is the shrinking of their circle of friends and family, schoolmates and work colleagues. Though the loss of loved ones is much the most difficult to bear, old age can sometimes be a time of repeated loss, when the job, role, status and abilities also seem to become things of the past. It takes resilience and determination to compensate for missing occupations and roles and to find an emotional outlet, and none of us is able to bounce back resourcefully all the time. All the same, it does seem that the happiest retirements are often the busiest, those of people who are involved with their families and communities and never lack a reason to get up and get on with life. Bereavement of a lifetime companion, close friend or relative is a different and more serious matter, however, and needs fuller consideration.

Coping after a death: the practical side

Not knowing what to do on these occasions adds to the distress of mourners. This section starts with a look at the formalities involved in funeral and other arrangements to be made after a death.

The death certificate

If the death occurs at home, the family doctor who looked after the person in their last illness will give a death certificate. This must be taken to the Registrar of Births and Deaths for the area within five days of the death. It is also possible to make a formal declaration giving all necessary information in any other register office, which will be passed on to the registrar for the area in which the death occurred. This may be helpful for someone who is trying to arrange a funeral from some distance away. The doctor should be able to tell you where the office is, or you can find it in the phone book or ask at the Citizens Advice Bureau. You may want to telephone in advance to make sure it is the right office and to check on hours of opening, and also to make sure that you have all the necessary documents and information to register the death.

If the death occurs in hospital, it is still necessary to take the death certificate to the registrar's office, but in this case it will be the office for the hospital area, not for the person's home. The hospital staff will be able to direct you to this when you collect the certificate.

The hospital doctors may want to perform a post-mortem examination on the dead person's body; in this case the closest relative will be asked for their consent. This is never pleasant to think about, but it may help to remember that doctors learn a lot about illnesses and their treatment from these procedures, and that some people would like to think they could give help to others even after their death.

The role of the coroner

Sometimes relatives are surprised and distressed to find that these routine procedures are delayed because the death has to be referred to the coroner. This is a person with legal and/or medical training whose job it is to enquire into the cause of a sudden, violent or unexpected death and to make sure that the registered cause of death is correct. There is some variation around the country as to which deaths have to be referred to the coroner, but in general they include those where the GP did not see the patient in the last illness or is unsure of the cause of death (perhaps when the death was sudden), those following an accident or surgical operation and those related to the person's previous employment or to drug or alcohol abuse. It is only very rarely that the coroner is involved because foul play is suspected; however, if you are worried about the referral, your own doctor should be able to tell you the cause of the delay.

The coroner may decide that a post-mortem is necessary, and the relatives cannot oppose this. If the death is then found to be due to natural causes, the coroner will issue a notification of this for the relative to take to the registrar. Occasionally, an inquest will be ordered; in this case it is best to get in touch with the coroner's office to check when a death certificate will be available and funeral arrangements may be made.

At the registrar's

Once the death is registered, the relative will be given two certificates, one white and one green. The white one contains a Social Security form to claim any remaining benefit due to the dead person's estate; this can also be used for the widow to claim her benefits. The green certificate allows burial or cremation to go ahead. Further copies of the death certificate can be purchased if needed, for instance to arrange probate and wind up the dead person's affairs (eg closing a bank account).

Arranging the funeral

If the death took place at home, the funeral director can remove the body as soon as the doctor has certified death; in hospital, he or she will collect it from the hospital mortuary. It is usual to ask for a quotation for the expenses of the funeral, perhaps including one for the basic funeral, and an itemised list of costs should be provided. If the person who is responsible for arranging a funeral is receiving a means-tested state benefit, they may be entitled to a payment towards the cost. Contact the local Benefits Agency for more information.

For further information, you may like to consult Age Concern's Factsheets 27 *Arranging a funeral* and 14 *Dealing with someone's estate*. The Citizens Advice Bureau will also be able to help.

After a death: the emotional side

Numbness

Recently bereaved people are often surprised at how little they feel in the early stages; they may go through the necessary practical tasks almost like robots, and this stage may last up to the funeral. During this time it is common to find it difficult to remember things, and to do things absent-mindedly, like squeezing toothpaste onto the razor rather than the toothbrush. This is just a sign of stress and distress, not of madness, and will pass in time.

The funeral

This is a very important 'rite of passage' in which those who were close to the dead person can express their pain, and support each other in the very beginnings of coming to terms with a world with their memory of the person rather than their presence. People who try to prevent frail or very elderly people from attending funerals often mean well, but their kindness is misplaced; the expression of grief is important and should be allowed to take its course.

It helps survivors if the service can be made to reflect something of the life and personality of the person who has died, perhaps by incorporating a favourite piece of music or by asking friends or colleagues to read poems or to recall memories of times together. Most clergy welcome suggestions of this sort and will be glad to advise. Some people also like to keep a memorial book for mourners to record their sympathy; this should be open at the church or chapel and at the reception afterwards. Letters and cards received can be added to make a very special memorial to an important and significant life.

After the funeral

This can be a difficult time, as supportive family and friends tend to withdraw support to pick up the threads of their own lives. During this time the bereaved person experiences a fairly constant sadness, with acute paroxysms of almost unbearable distress. These are often brought on by a sudden reminder of the loss, such as a letter addressed to 'Mr and Mrs' or a favourite tune.

Sorting through the deceased's possessions is bound to be distressing. It is best not to embark on this too soon, when the tendency to get rid of everything that carries a memory may be regretted later. Gentle help in this sad task is very valuable, with the most bereaved person being encouraged to decide general policy and others concerning themselves with the detail. When unsure whether to dispose of things, it is always wise to postpone the decision to a less sensitive time.

Unexpected and unpleasant feelings

Relationships are never perfect: old misunderstandings can be handed down in families from one generation to another; the origins and the consequences of actions may not become clear until some time after the event. For all these reasons, emotions such as anger and guilt may be as prominent as grief. The anger may be directed at anyone who is nearby: the doctors, nurses and other professionals who were unable to prevent the death; relatives and others who may be thought to be neglectful; or God in the case of a religious person. Where there has been apparent negligence, it is important to lodge a complaint, but in most cases the anger is part of a cry of pain. You may be taken by surprise at the strength of these feelings; try to remember that they are as natural and appropriate as the more expected sadness, and that they will fade away in time.

A feeling of guilt shows itself in many ways; a common one is to think of ways the story could have ended 'if only' this or that had been done. This is unhelpful; it is never possible to be sure of the consequences of what we do, and living each hour as if it were our last is not a practical proposition. It is better to concentrate on the solidity of the underlying relationship and the sustained understanding behind it. There is always an element of 'survivor guilt' among those close to the death, and this too should be expected and endured.

Resolution

After some time – often as long as a year in a close relationship – those who were left behind start to put together a new life containing the dead person's memory though not their physical presence. This is right and proper, and no one should feel guilty the first time they 'forget' the bereavement long enough to enjoy themselves for a while. There will continue to be relapses at anniversaries of significant dates: birthdays, Christmas, wedding anniversaries and the anniversaries of the death and funeral. It is sensible to arrange to be in the loving company of people who know and care for you and sympathise with your distress at these times. New losses may also stimulate unfinished grieving and evoke renewed distress. Eventually, reminders of the dead person will no longer be painful and will evoke only happy memories.

Helping a bereaved person: some dos and don'ts

- Don't be tempted to avoid them; many bereaved people report this as being particularly hard to bear.
- Don't expect to feel good after a visit to a house of mourning; if one person is to receive comfort, another often has to give it up.
- Don't expect a bereaved person to be pleasant; they are often touchy, and you may find it easy to say the wrong thing; be slow to take offence yourself.
- Don't worry that you don't know what to say: there are no magic words to put things right. Say how sorry you are, and encourage the bereaved person to talk if they wish; if not, be tolerant of silence.
- Do offer practical help, if you are able to; taking the dog for a walk, doing some shopping or undertaking to feed the cat may be a great help to someone caught in the unaccustomed bustle of funeral arrangements. The offer of a plate of sandwiches for the mourners after the funeral may also be well received. Later it may be useful to put the bereaved person in touch with one of the organisations that help mourners. These include the National Association of Bereavement

Services, CRUSE – Bereavement Care and the Lesbian and Gay Bereavement Project; they often have local support groups, and also offer counselling and practical advice, as do some local groups/organisations of Age Concern (see the 'Useful addresses' section for contact details).

■ Do write a letter; the thought that the dead person touched many lives for good is often a great comfort. Memories of good times with or kind actions by them are especially useful.

■ Do be selective in what you say; speaking ill of the dead is usually a mistake, however unsatisfactory they were when they were alive. A neutral remark like 'you must miss him dreadfully' is safer. However, don't be tempted to praise to the skies untruthfully; if it was a long and happy marriage, by all means say so; if it was not, say nothing.

The death of someone we love is probably the worst thing that happens to most of us. However, it is the price we pay for loving relationships; grieving is sad, but it would be far worse to have nothing and nobody to mourn for.

Enjoying retirement

However welcome it may seem when under pressure in a busy working life, retirement always involves a complete change of lifestyle. More time for family and friends and to pursue interests and hobbies may be welcome, but the lack of structure to the day and the loss of the companionship of workmates may present difficulties. If possible, try to prepare for your retirement by attending a pre-retirement course. A graded retirement, moving from full-time to part-time working before giving up altogether often seems to make the changeover easier. You may also want to consider the options for voluntary work, study and other activities set out on pages 24–26.

Women or men whose work has been mainly in the home are not exempt from the effect of change. Over the years they will have evolved a lifestyle pattern that did not include the partner. People approach times like these with preconceived ideas about the amount of time to be spent together, and a great deal of discussion and negotiation may be needed before the two of them can dovetail their days into a rearranged life pattern.

Retirement may be a less happy time than anticipated if care is not taken. People with a family history of depressive illness, or those who have had episodes of depression before, need to be especially careful around the time of retirement, as life events of this sort can precipitate a new episode. Below are some suggestions for preventing problems of this sort.

- Find a way of occupying yourself and adding structure to your day.
- Try to maintain a circle of friends and acquaintances, perhaps by picking up the threads with some of the people on your Christmas card list or by getting to know new contacts better. You may want to keep in touch with your closest workmates, but do not expect too much; it may be more difficult to find topics of common interest once you spend your days apart.
- Find a confidant among family and friends if possible; it is very helpful to 'de-brief' and shed life's little irritations as well as major troubles.
- After a working life spent managing or caring for other people, it can be very difficult to admit to a need for help oneself, perhaps with relationships that are under strain in changed circumstances; don't let false pride get in the way of putting things right with a counsellor or other professional.
- Take care of your physical health; there is a strong connection between illness and depression. Collect up your old tablets and take them to the doctor for review – some may no longer be needed, and unwanted effects are more likely to occur as you get older.
- Organise some body maintenance: have your eyes, teeth and feet checked.
- Make sure you have things to look forward to: small ones daily, and bigger ones at longer intervals.
- Reflect on your past life and try to resolve any painful conflicts. This may involve visiting old haunts, making up old quarrels, or forgiving yourself for the sorts of mistakes that are part of being human. Everyone has to find their own peace in their own way, and time spent on this is not wasted.

CHAPTER 3

Illness and Disability in Later Life

Illness and disability are not normal at any time of life; there is always a cause or a number of contributory factors at the root of the trouble. Advancing age may make a person more vulnerable to a disease and slower to recover, but is never the only explanation for pain, disability and loss of function. This chapter gives brief details of some common health problems affecting older people, describes the medical treatment available and suggests some ways in which you can help yourself. You may also like to refer to the list of helpful organisations on pages 131–144.

Do not be tempted to use this information for self-diagnosis, as this can lead to unnecessary worry and distress. However, knowing the facts should increase your confidence in discussing your care with your doctors. To make the best use of consultation time, note down questions you want to ask or particular worries that you have, and take a list with you. Do not feel intimidated; doctors are just ordinary people with some specialised knowledge, and many are delighted to meet well-informed patients who want to take some responsibility for their own health.

Occasionally, you may be unlucky enough to be asked 'What do you expect at your age?' Be prepared with the answers. First, you should expect a fair hearing as you describe your symptoms and the ways in which they interfere with your life. Secondly, you should be offered a physical examination if appropriate, and whatever tests are necessary to establish the cause of your problem. Thirdly, you should be given a clear explanation of what is happening to you, your likely future outlook and an outline of possible lines of treatment. Fourthly, you should be given appropriate help whenever this is possible; this may involve a prescription from the doctor, advice on helpful lifestyle changes or a referral to another specialist or to another professional such as a physiotherapist or dietitian. Be polite but persistent in asking for explanations and help, and take care to make your preferences known. You have too much experience of life to expect miracles, but your hard-working life has entitled you to the same sort of health care as the rest of the community.

How the health system works

General practitioners (GPs) are the usual starting point for someone with health problems. They often work with nurses, health visitors, physiotherapists, occupational therapists, speech and language therapists, chiropodists, dietitians, counsellors and other staff, to form the 'primary health care team'. They are responsible for meeting their patients' day-to-day health needs, providing the first line of treatment and referring patients on for hospital treatment.

Everyone is entitled to a GP. If you need to find one because you have moved to a new area, you can obtain a list of local doctors from the public library, main post office, Citizens Advice Bureau, local community health council and local health authority (addresses can be found in the telephone book). You can find out more about any GP practice you are considering by visiting it and asking to see a copy of the practice leaflet. If English is not your first language, you may want to choose a doctor who speaks your language, or find a practice with a link worker who shares your ethnic background; you could also ask for a copy of the practice leaflet in your mother tongue. You may also prefer to see a doctor of the same sex as yourself.

Once you have decided on the doctor you prefer, you can go to the surgery and ask to be registered; take your medical card with you if possible. You may find that the doctor's list is already full, as is sometimes the case with a popular practice. If you have trouble finding a doctor who can accept you, get in touch with the health authority, who will find a GP for you.

If you want to change your doctor, you should approach the new practice and apply to be registered, as outlined above. You do not have to tell the old practice you are leaving why you are going, but it can be helpful if you do so.

GPs are able to remove patients from their list without giving a reason but this seems to be a rare event. Doctors are encouraged by their professional organisations to discuss a problem situation with the patient concerned.

Few GPs now work on their own, so you can arrange to see any doctor in the practice or health centre – not necessarily the one with whom you are registered. For instance, if an internal examination is needed or you want to discuss an intimate problem, you might prefer to see a doctor of the same sex as yourself. Also, if the treatment you are offered is unsuitable for your religion or cultural background, do make your difficulties known; a relative with language skills or a religious leader might be able to help with this.

It is up to the doctor where, and how urgently, you are seen. If you think you need a home visit, it is often useful to discuss your illness with the doctor direct over the telephone. The practice may have a special time for telephone consultations, or may make arrangements for the doctor to telephone you.

A practice or health centre provides 24-hour cover for the patients on its list, and how this is done will be described in the practice leaflet. Some-times the doctors in the practice will work out-of-hours on a rota, or they may form a co-operative with doctors from other practices nearby, or they may employ a deputising service. It is wise to keep a note of the emergency number for calls out of hours, and to have a pen and paper to hand when telephoning in case you are referred on to a further number. Illness is no respecter of the clock or calendar, and medical attention may be necessary at any time of the day or night. However, an emergency ser-vice cannot provide continuing care from a doctor who knows you, so, whenever possible, it is sensible to see your doctor during normal prac-tice hours.

If you think you need a second opinion about your health from another GP, you should discuss this with your own doctor. Similarly, you may think it would help to see a hospital specialist. In both cases the decision is the doctor's, but polite persistence by you will probably be rewarded.

If you need to go into hospital, you may be sent an information booklet before admission, and this will probably answer many of your queries.

You are entitled to information about your condition, its treatment and the outlook for the future. Once in hospital, if you find it difficult to ask questions when the doctor is on the 'ward round', ask the senior nurse to arrange for you to see the doctor privately at another time. If you need an operation, you will be asked to sign a 'consent form' agreeing to the procedure; this is a good opportunity to make sure you understand why the operation is necessary and what its effects will be as well as any risks. In teaching hospitals, medical students gain experience in talking to patients and learning how to examine them, and this is a great help to the doctors and patients of tomorrow. However, you do not have to be seen by students, and you should tell the nurse in charge if you prefer not to. You are, of course, free to refuse any kind of treatment, and are free to leave the hospital at any time, but you may be asked to sign a form to say that you do this against medical advice.

If you feel you have grounds for complaint, it is sensible to start by discussing the problem with the practice manager or with the doctor direct. If this does not put things right, the next step is to ask the health authority to have your complaint sent for independent review. If you are still not satisfied, your complaint can be referred to the Health Service Ombudsman. You can get help in using the complaints system from the community health council or the health authority (find them in the telephone directory).

Further information can be found in Age Concern's Factsheet 44 *Family doctors and their services.*

Some common illnesses

This section discusses common illnesses and problems in alphabetical order.

Anaemia

What it is Anaemia is a lack of the red pigment called haemoglobin, which carries vital oxygen round the body and supplies it to all the tissues. It may lead to breathlessness, tiredness or, in extreme cases, to apathy and self-neglect. However, anaemia may be discovered by accident during investigations for other reasons. Skin colour is a poor guide; many fair-skinned people have normal blood.

Why it happens A common reason for anaemia is unnoticed leaking of blood from the lining of the gut, due to piles, inflammation of the gullet (reflux oesophagitis), a peptic ulcer, diverticulitis (discussed later) or, more seriously, a bowel cancer. Leakage is more common in people who take some medication called NSAIDs (non-steroidal anti-inflammatory drugs – eg ibuprofen) for arthritis. Another cause is poor nutrition, especially lack of iron or of folate (folic acid), or poor absorption of nutrients from the bowel. Pernicious anaemia is the serious form, which happens when vitamin B_{12} cannot be absorbed; if untreated, it can cause nerve damage and mental confusion, but regular injections of the missing vitamin can prevent these.

How your doctor can help Your doctor will have blood tests done to detect anaemia and identify its cause. Appropriate treatment can then be prescribed.

Helping yourself If you suspect that you may be bleeding into your gut because your stools are black and tarry or contain obvious blood, you should see your doctor, both to have the cause put right and to correct the possible anaemia.

Try to include some iron-rich foods in your diet, such as liver and kidney (once a week), red meat and oily fish (three or four times a week). Fortified cereals, spinach, beans, lentils, eggs, dried fruit and tofu contain lesser amounts. Vitamin C-rich drinks such as orange juice increase iron absorption; this may be useful to know if you do not eat meat. If you are a strict vegetarian who takes no animal products, you may want to ask your doctor whether you need an iron supplement; it is unwise to take iron without medical advice.

The best sources of folate are liver and kidneys, whole-grain cereals, nuts and pulses; green-leafed vegetables contain a lesser amount, while fruits are a comparatively poor source. Folate is destroyed by prolonged heating in water.

Angina

What it is Angina is tight, frightening chest pain, usually brought on by exercise or emotion, and lasting only a few minutes.

Why it happens It happens when insufficient blood reaches the heart muscle because the coronary arteries are narrowed by fatty 'fur' called *atheroma*. People from the Indian sub-continent are especially likely to have coronary heart disease of this sort.

How your doctor can help Your doctor will probably prescribe glyceryl trinitrate (GTN) tablets or spray to expand (dilate) the blood vessels and relieve attacks by improving the blood supply to the heart muscle. Frequent attacks can be prevented by daily treatment with drugs called beta-blockers or calcium channel blockers. Surgical treatment includes stretching a narrowed artery (angioplasty), or diverting blood through a new passage using a blood vessel taken from elsewhere in the body (coronary artery bypass graft or CABG – pronounced 'cabbage').

Helping yourself Stop smoking; avoid being overweight; visit the doctor regularly to monitor your blood pressure, and take treatment if it is high; eat small amounts of animal fats and plenty of fruit and vegetables; take exercise.

Further information about heart disease is available from the British Heart Foundation (address on p 134).

Arterial disease

What it is Narrowed arteries supply insufficient blood to the muscles of the leg for their needs. This causes pain in the calf or further up the leg, sometimes with 'pins and needles' and tenderness in the toes. In milder cases this happens only on exercise, but in more severe ones symptoms occur at rest. In the worst cases, where there is insufficient blood to keep the tissues healthy, gangrene can develop.

Why it happens The arteries tend to 'fur up' with atheroma as we grow older, but this process is quicker and more severe in people who smoke, take little exercise, eat a poor diet or have diabetes.

How your doctor can help Your doctor will order tests to find the scale of the problem, treat conditions such as anaemia and diabetes that make things worse, and prescribe pain-killers if you need them. Surgery may be advisable in more severe cases. Special X-rays called arteriograms are used to map out the vessels, after which they may be stretched, unblocked or bypassed by grafts. The few people who develop gangrene may need amputation.

Helping yourself Change your lifestyle if necessary. Try to prevent injury to the fragile skin of your feet, as this will heal poorly, and visit a chiropodist regularly. A slightly higher shoe heel may relax your calf muscle and help your pain.

Arthritis

There are three main types of arthritis: the commonest is osteoarthritis, which affects nearly 70 per cent of women and nearly 60 per cent of men over 65 years old.

Osteoarthritis

What it is Certain changes in the cartilage of joints cause pain and stiffness and restrict activity.

Why it happens Osteoarthritis runs in families to some extent, and joints that are already damaged seem most likely to be affected. Abnormal wear and tear and being overweight make things worse.

How your doctor can help Your doctor will prescribe pain-killers; he or she can also refer you for physiotherapy to strengthen your muscles or for an operation to replace an arthritic joint.

Helping yourself Lose weight if necessary. Keep active and try putting all your joints through their full range of movement every morning, perhaps with instruction from a physiotherapist if necessary. Do not force a painful joint, though; exercise should not hurt. Improve your daily living skills by using walking aids or other equipment to make tasks easier and improve your independence; a physiotherapist or occupational therapist can advise you about this. Use heated pads or cold packs if they help to relieve your pain.

Rheumatoid arthritis

What it is Rheumatoid arthritis is a disease that affects joints by attacking the lining membrane, and which also affects other tissues in the body. It is more common in women, usually starting in their 30s or 40s but can begin in older people. The joints of the hands and feet are usually affected first; they become hot, swollen and painful. After several attacks, permanent damage can lead to joint deformity and restricted function.

Why it happens The cause is not well understood.

How your doctor can help The doctor will prescribe drugs to relieve pain, to reduce inflammation or to modify the disease, and will treat problems outside the joints as they arise. He or she may suggest referring you to a specialist.

Helping yourself You should aim for a balance of rest and exercise; physiotherapy and use of equipment for daily living as suggested by a physiotherapist or occupational therapist may also be helpful.

Gout

What it is Crystals form within a joint and irritate its lining, so the joint becomes inflamed, red, shiny and very tender. First attacks often affect a single joint such as the one at the base of the great toe, but later attacks may involve several joints.

How your doctor can help Prescribed drugs can relieve the pain and inflammation and also prevent further attacks.

Helping yourself Gout is not necessarily a sign of high living but, if you are advised to change your diet or to drink less alcohol, it is wise to do so.

The self-help organisation for all sorts of arthritis is Arthritis Care (for the address, see p 132).

Asthma

What it is Asthma causes attacks of cough, chest 'tightness' and wheezing. The attacks come about because the tubes (called *airways* or *bronchi*) that conduct the air to and from the depths of the lungs become narrowed. This happens because the muscle of the airway wall goes into spasm, the lining swells and thick mucus is secreted into the centre of the tube; there is then less space for air to pass.

Why it happens Various triggers can bring on an attack of asthma. These include infections, exercise, emotional factors, cold dry air, cigarette smoke, fumes and drugs such as aspirin, beta-blockers and the non-steroidal anti-inflammatory agents (eg ibuprofen) used to treat conditions such as arthritis. Allergy to pet hair, pollen or the house dust-mite is less common as a cause in older people.

How your doctor can help Your doctor will first make certain of the diagnosis, because other conditions can have symptoms like those of asthma. Having listened to your story of your symptoms and looked at a chest X-ray, the doctor might decide to check your lung function from day to day and even in the course of the day, as variations are typical of asthma. To do this means using a peak flow meter, which measures the maximum rate at which you can breathe out when blowing as hard and as fast as possible. Another test involves your taking a two-week course of steroids: if you have asthma, the peak flow will improve by 15 per cent or more.

Treatment for asthma involves two sorts of drugs:

- those taken regularly every day, to prevent attacks;
- those taken only during attacks, to relieve the symptoms.

Steroids, often taken through an inhaler, are examples of drugs used for prevention; 'reliever' drugs include salbutamol and terbutaline. The doctor will prescribe suitable medicines and follow you up to make sure they are effective.

Helping yourself Learn enough about your condition to be a well-informed partner in your care. Good sources of information include the National Asthma Campaign and the British Lung Foundation (see pp 139 and 134). Learn to recognise when your asthma is getting worse, and remember to seek medical help during an attack:

- if the effects of your 'reliever' drug last less than four hours;
- if breathing is very difficult;
- if your lips become bluish;
- if your pulse is very fast;

■ if your peak flow reading is less than half what it usually is;
■ if you feel exhausted by the attack.

Broken bones (fractures)

What they are The commonest bones to break are the hip (neck of the femur), the wrist (Colles' fracture) and the vertebrae of the spine, which are squashed into 'crush fractures'. A broken limb is usually swollen, very painful, difficult to move and may look an abnormal shape. There may also be a grating noise as the two broken ends scrape against each other; however, this should not be made to happen deliberately, because nearby tissues such as nerves can be badly damaged.

Why they happen Falls are common causes of fractures. Fit, active older people whose fractures are caused by simple accidents usually do well. Frail older people may fall because of illness, which complicates and slows recovery. Women are affected more severely than men by osteoporosis, and their weaker bones break more easily than men's.

How your doctor can help If you break your hip, you will usually have an operation to replace the broken-off piece of bone by an artificial part. You will be able to take a few steps, with help, the day after the operation. The geriatric–orthopaedic team of therapists, doctors and nurses will work together to get you back to your normal level of activity, and home adaptations and equipment may be arranged to help you regain your independence at home.

A Colles' fracture is usually 'reduced' (that is, the bones are put back into their proper position) under anaesthetic. They are then held still by a plaster cast so that they heal correctly.

Helping yourself Prevention is better than cure! Refer to the section on osteoporosis on page 72 for tips on keeping your bones strong. You can minimise your chances of falling by being sensibly careful around your home, without reducing your enjoyment of a full active life (see p 111 for suggestions). After a fracture, you can speed your return to independent living by co-operating with rehabilitation and following medical advice about activity; a heat pad and pain-killers will make this easier and more comfortable.

Cancers

What they are Normally the body's cells divide in an orderly way to repair tissues or to grow according to the needs of the whole body. When cells become cancerous, they over-grow to form lumps; 'tumour' is another word for lump. *Benign* tumours affect only the parts of the body immediately around them; they can usually be removed and will not come back. Warts are benign tumours. *Malignant* tumours are more serious, because they invade and destroy the healthy tissues around them, and can spread to distant parts of the body along blood or lymph vessels. 'Cancer' is the popular name for malignant tumours, but it is not helpful to think of it as a single disease. There are many different kinds, and the prospects for people with cancer are very much better than they used to be, with one in three being completely cured. This is partly because modern tests mean that the diagnosis can be made earlier, and partly because methods of treatment are improving all the time.

Why they happen Some cancers are caused by irritant substances, such as the tobacco smoke that causes lung cancer. There also seems to be a link between cancers of the bowel and the respiratory system and a shortage of fruit and vegetables in the diet. High doses of radiation are also implicated in a few cases, and family background may contribute to others. In many cases of cancer, however, no obvious cause is found. On the whole, people from the Indian sub-continent are less vulnerable to cancer; so are Afro-Caribbeans, except for prostate cancer.

How your doctor can help Once cancer is suspected, tests are performed to find out whether it is there and, if so, what sort it is, how malignant it is and whether it has spread to form 'secondaries' away from the original ('primary') growth. A sample of the suspect tissue, called a biopsy, is often taken so that it can be examined under the microscope, and scans, blood tests and sometimes exploratory operations assess the degree of spread.

There are three common sorts of treatment used for cancer: surgery, radiotherapy and chemotherapy (drug treatment). They may be used separately or in any combination, and which plan is best will vary from one person to another. The object of surgery is to remove the original or 'primary' growth before it causes severe local damage, and if possible before it has had a chance to spread (metastasise) to produce secondary deposits (metastases) in other parts of the body. Radiotherapy and cytotoxic drugs act in the same way: they kill rapidly dividing cells. The usefulness of these treatments depends on the fact that cancerous cells divide more quickly than normal ones, and are therefore killed before them. Some drug treatment involves hormones; the principle is to block or oppose the action of the hormone that helps tumours of such organs as the prostate gland, ovary or breast to grow.

Helping yourself People with cancer vary in how much they want to know about their illness and its treatment, so you should ask your doctor for all the information you need to understand what is happening to you. It may also help to get in touch with a patient support group such as Cancer BACUP or Cancerlink, or the groups that concentrate on particular types of cancer, such as that of the breast. Your mental and spiritual state are also important, and you may want to talk with a religious leader or receive counselling. Friends may suggest you try complementary therapy as well as your more orthodox treatment. Remember that techniques such as aromatherapy, reflexology or yoga may well improve your feelings of well-being, but there is no evidence that they have any effect on the course of the cancer, and you should be very wary of any unorthodox form of treatment that seems to offer a cure. Some forms of complementary therapy are unsuitable for people with particular types of cancer or undergoing radiotherapy, so it is wise to check with your doctor as to what is suitable for you.

Types of cancer

Breast Signs Changes in the look or feel of the breast, a lump in the breast or armpit, skin dimpling or an in-turned or discharging nipple. **Investigations** Careful examination, mammography (see p 21) and biopsy. **Treatment** Surgery tends to be less mutilating than it used to be, and removal of the whole breast (mastectomy) is not always necessary; when it is, breast reconstruction may be possible. Radiotherapy may be given after the operation, and drugs such as tamoxifen used to prevent regrowth. **Helpful organisation** Breast Cancer Care.

Bladder *Signs* Blood in the urine, repeated urinary infections or pain in the lower abdomen and private parts. **Investigations** The bladder lining can be inspected through a cystoscope – a thin telescope that is passed into the bladder through its drainage tube (the urethra) under anaesthetic. The tumour can usually be removed surgically through the cystoscope, and drugs or radiotherapy may also be used. The cystoscopies are repeated at intervals for the rest of the patient's life, to check that the cancer has not recurred.

Bowel *Signs* Bleeding from the back passage or passing of black, tarry stools that contain partially digested blood; change in bowel habit, with unusual episodes of constipation or diarrhoea. **Investigations** A barium enema, in which barium that shows up on X-ray (contrast medium) is put into the bowel through the back passage. It then outlines the bowel lining and shows up any abnormality. The bowel can also be looked at directly through a thin telescope called a colonoscope or a sigmoidoscope, and a piece of tissue can be taken for testing. CT scans are also increasingly used. **Treatment** A bowel cancer is usually removed surgically; if possible the two cut ends of the bowel are joined together so that stools can be passed into the lavatory in the usual way. When this cannot be done, a colostomy is formed – an opening is made on the abdominal wall, through which the bowel empties into a bag. **Helpful organisation** British Colostomy Association.

Cervix and womb (the cervix is the narrow 'neck' that forms the entrance to the womb) **Signs** Abnormal vaginal bleeding, either starting again in a woman past the menopause or between periods in a younger woman. Cervical cancer or pre-cancer sometimes shows up on a cervical smear in a woman without symptoms. **Investigations** Further sampling of tissue for laboratory examination; this usually involves a biopsy of the cervix or scraping the lining of the womb. Examination under anaesthetic or scans may be performed to try to find out whether the tumour has spread. **Treatment** This aims to kill the abnormal cells by laser, surgery, radiotherapy or a combination of these. The radiation may be provided by a radium implant; to get the right dose, this is inserted under anaesthetic and left in place for a measured number of hours before being removed.

Leukaemia *Signs* Anaemia, vulnerability to infections and abnormal bleeding; there may be no symptoms, so the condition is often found by chance on a routine blood test. The abnormal cells circulate in the blood, so swellings occur only if the liver, spleen or lymph nodes become invaded. *Investigations* Samples of blood or bone marrow are taken and examined under the microscope. *Treatment* Cytotoxic drugs are often used; some types of leukaemia in older people progress very slowly, so treatment may be deferred until the disease shows signs of becoming more active.

Lung *Signs* A persisting cough, especially with blood in the sputum (spit), a chest infection that is slow to clear, shortness of breath or chest pain, especially when the person is a smoker. *Investigations* Chest X-ray, then examination of a spit sample for abnormal cells (cytology), or sampling of the tumour under anaesthetic through a telescope called a bronchoscope passed down the windpipe. *Treatment* Radiotherapy to shrink tumours that are causing pressure symptoms, pain or bleeding. Surgery to remove the tumour is rarely possible in older people.

Prostate gland *Signs* This results in the same difficulties in passing water as with benign (harmless) enlargement of the gland (see p 74). *Investigations* The size of the gland can be assessed on rectal (back passage) examination, and the presence of a cancer is shown by blood tests, a needle biopsy, X-rays and scans. *Treatment* This varies from one man to another. Many tumours grow so slowly that it is best to observe their progress and start treatment only if it becomes necessary. Such treatment may then involve surgery, radiotherapy or drugs. As prostate cancer depends on the male hormone testosterone to help it grow, hormone treatment opposing its action is often effective; in some cases the testicles, which are the source of testosterone, may be removed.

Skin *Signs* Skin tumours usually form lumps, warty masses, or persisting ulcers that fail to heal. The commonest type is the rodent ulcer, usually found on the face. The much rarer malignant melanoma looks like a mole that has grown bigger and may bleed. *Investigations* A tissue sample is examined under the microscope. *Treatment* Surgical removal is commonest, but radiotherapy can be used. Either usually produces a complete cure of the rodent ulcer but the malignant melanoma commonly recurs.

Chest infections

What they are These are infections that are named according to the part of the breathing apparatus affected by the inflammation, or '-itis'. Tracheitis affects the windpipe (trachea) and causes a cough and soreness behind the breastbone, while acute bronchitis affects the lung's large airways (bronchi) and results in a 'wet' cough with thick green or yellow spit. Inflammation and infection of the lungs themselves is pneumonitis or pneumonia. This may cause a cough with chest pain, but the most noticeable abnormality in some very elderly people may be mental confusion and a tendency to fall. Chest infections are diagnosed by careful examination of the chest, sometimes with a chest X-ray or identification of the bacteria in the spit.

Why they happen Chest infections are often a complication of colds or flu; smokers get them more often than non-smokers.

How your doctor can help Your doctor will help by prescribing antibiotics and/or medicines to make breathing easier, and, if you are a smoker, by supporting your decision to stop.

Helping yourself If you smoke, stop at once. Stay in the warm and drink plenty of fluids. Steam inhalations may make the spit easier to cough up, but be careful of scalding from the hot water.

Chronic bronchitis and emphysema

What they are Someone with chronic bronchitis has repeated chest infections, when the colour of the spit (mucus) brought up by their cough changes from white or clear to green or yellow. Emphysema often affects the same people; it causes progressive destruction of lung tissue, so the person becomes short of oxygen and gets breathless on exercise.

Why they happen A tendency to these diseases may run in families, and is made worse by smoking, air pollution, dusty occupations and exposure to infection, such as colds or flu. People of Irish extraction are especially vulnerable to chronic (long-term) chest disease.

How your doctor can help Your doctor will prescribe antibiotics to kill the bacteria causing the infection, and bronchodilators to expand the airways (bronchi)and ease breathing. Flu vaccinations should be given each autumn. The self-help organisation for these conditions is the British Lung Foundation (address on p 134).

Helping yourself Stop smoking; press for clean air.

Colds

What they are The sore throat, sneezing and runny nose that becomes blocked are well known to us all.

Why they happen Colds are caused by infection with one of many different sorts of virus.

How your doctor can help An uncomplicated cold cannot be treated by antibiotics. It is not usually necessary to consult the doctor unless you develop complications such as a chest infection, or if your cold is slow to go away.

Helping yourself Try not to spread your cold around. If possible, keep away from other people during the early sneezing stage, when it is most infectious. Careful handwashing also helps to prevent spread. Take paracetamol for discomfort, drink plenty of fluids and keep warm. You may find hot lemon or blackcurrant drinks comforting. Steam inhalations may help to clear your head, but take care not to scald yourself with the hot water.

Constipation

What it is Constipation is the difficult, painful and infrequent passage of hard stools. It should be reported to the doctor if the bowel habit has changed, or if there is bleeding from the back passage, as these can be early signs of bowel cancer.

Why it happens Ageing bowel muscle works more slowly, so it takes longer for food to travel the length of the gut; this is made worse if the diet lacks fibre and/or fluids. Medicines such as pain-killers and cough medicines may further slow bowel action, as may lack of exercise. If piles or a fissure make opening the bowels painful, the person may try to avoid it, so the stools get even harder, passing them is more painful and a vicious circle is set up.

How your doctor can help The doctor will help by giving you a medical check if necessary; by prescribing laxatives and/or enemas; and by providing lifestyle advice to prevent recurrence.

Helping yourself Eat a high-fibre diet with plentiful fluids, have adequate exercise and take as few constipating drugs as possible. One of the commonest drugs to have this unwanted effect is codeine, often found as an ingredient in pain-killers. Before buying such medicines over the counter, you might like to ask the pharmacist which ones are most suitable for someone with a tendency to constipation.

Deafness

What it is Deafness is hearing loss severe enough to make group conversation difficult, to interfere with hearing the doorbell or telephone or to make it necessary to turn up the sound on the TV or radio so loud that other people complain.

Why it happens Presbyacusis – literally 'old hearing' – affects the nervous tissue of the ear. Although it becomes more common as the years pass, experts are divided about whether it is simply due to ageing; noise damage, infections and some medicines seem to worsen it. Another cause of nerve deafness is Ménière's disease, which also affects balance. Nerve deafness is sometimes called *perceptive* or *sensori-neural* deafness; it cannot be cured but the affected person can be helped to make the most of their remaining hearing. The causes of *conductive* deafness in the outer and middle parts of the ear can sometimes be put right; examples are the removal of earwax by drops and/or syringing, and surgery to correct defects in the tiny bones of the middle ear.

How your doctor can help The doctor or the practice nurse can examine your ears and remove wax if this seems to be contributing to the problem. If you are still deaf, you should ask to be referred to the hearing clinic of the local hospital, where an accurate diagnosis can be made and treatment planned.

Helping yourself Hearing services are under considerable pressure, and you may find that a degree of polite persistence is necessary before you can receive help. If the surgery is quiet, the doctor may underestimate the difficulties you experience in noisier surroundings, and you may need to point this out. A friend with unimpaired hearing may be useful as escort to the hospital. As well as providing moral support, he or she can help if you need to ask for directions from staff who lack experience with hearing loss.

After your consultation, you may be prescribed a hearing aid. These amplify sound, but cannot correct the distortion some people experience. NHS models are satisfactory for most people's needs, but in some areas you may have to wait for one to be supplied. Hearing aids may also be bought privately but even those advertised as hearing 'correctors' or 'adjusters' are still only amplifying hearing aids. Some privately bought aids are less obtrusive than NHS models and may have other small advantages, but it is important to remember that they can be expensive to buy. Further, the purchase price may not cover the costs of repairs and maintenance, so running costs have to be added to the original purchase price. Hire purchase terms may be on offer, but you may want to check with the Citizens Advice Bureau or a knowledgeable relative or friend before signing an agreement.

NHS aids always come with an explanatory booklet, and more information can also be found in two publications from the Royal National Institute for Deaf People (RNID), *Hearing Aids – Questions and Answers* and *Understanding Hearing Aids* (for the address, see p 143).

Your local hearing clinic may have an attached hearing therapist, whose job is to help people to adjust to hearing loss and to get the best out of an aid. This can require a lot of effort. Many people do not realise until they wear one that a hearing aid amplifies background noise as well as conversation. If the person has not heard loudly and clearly for a while, the sudden din can be upsetting and difficult to cope with. This is why it is best to start using a new aid in a quiet room, with a companion who sits about six feet away with a good light on their face so that their lip movements are easy to see. When you progress to group conversation, you will need to turn the aid down in noisy surroundings such as a coffee morning or when meeting friends in the pub. The T switch on the aid enables it to receive magnetic signals from adapted telephones, TV sets and 'loop' systems installed in public buildings such as churches and theatres. You may want to consider installing a loop system at home; for more information about this and hearing impairment in general, contact the RNID or Hearing. Concern (addresses on pp 143 and 137).

Depressive illness

What it is This is a mental illness that the person cannot help. Features include low spirits, worse in the morning; poor sleep with early waking; slowness of mind and body; poor concentration; preoccupation with gloomy thoughts; agitation and indecision; and physical symptoms. In severe cases, there may be self-neglect and even self-harm with suicide attempts. Depressive illness is quite different from the normal variations in mood that everyone experiences from time to time; the feeling is more like despair, thinking and body function are disturbed as well as mood, and the person is quite unable to 'snap out of it'.

Why it happens It is more common in people with a family background of depression or an unhappy or abusive childhood. Poor health or social circumstances make it more likely to happen, especially in people who are isolated and lack a confidant. Loss of a loved one, a home or a role in life may trigger an episode of depression in someone with the tendency.

How your doctor can help Treatment involves a combination of action to improve social circumstances, 'talking therapies' such as psychotherapy or counselling, and medical treatment with drugs. Usually all three types of treatment are used at different stages of the illness. ECT (electroconvulsive therapy) is occasionally used in severe depression when drugs fail, but the increasing range of new, effective medicines with fewer side (unwanted) effects mean this is rarely needed now. Suicidal thoughts or actions should always be taken seriously and reported to the doctor, as severely depressed people are at real risk of self-harm.

Helping yourself Severe or persistent depression needs professional help. However, people who are affected may be unable to organise this for themselves without the help of friends and family, who may need to set the wheels in motion on their behalf.

If you are trying to keep depressive illness at bay yourself, it helps to take charge of your life, to keep busy and to find company, especially a confidant. Other recommendations include improving your health and social circumstances if possible, trying to compensate for any losses you may experience, and thinking positively. (See p 37 for further details of self-help measures.)

Information leaflets about depressive illness are available from the Royal College of Psychiatrists (address on p 142).

Diabetes

What it is Diabetes is the lack of insulin (called Type 1, or insulin-dependent diabetes mellitus, or IDDM) or insensitivity to it (Type 2, or non-insulin-dependent diabetes mellitus, or NIDDM). Without effective insulin, a person cannot process (metabolise) glucose from food properly. In older people, Type 2 is more common. It can lead to complications such as poor sight, incontinence, poor healing of foot injuries and of wounds in general, a liability to skin infections and increased likelihood of stroke and heart attack. These problems are often what take the affected person to the doctor.

Type 1 diabetes often starts in adolescence and can cause a severe illness, with violent thirst, passage of large amounts of urine, weight loss and sometimes coma.

Why it happens A tendency to develop diabetes may be inherited; it is especially common in older people from the Indian sub-continent and, to a lesser extent, in Afro-Caribbeans. Poor diet and lack of exercise make things worse. Diabetes is occasionally caused by alcohol abuse or the effects of gall bladder disease.

How your doctor can help Your doctor will help by referring you for advice about diet and/or prescribing tablets or insulin injections and by monitoring your health carefully so that any complications can be spotted early and dealt with at once.

Helping yourself Follow treatment instructions carefully; carry sugar and identification if you are subject to 'hypos' (low-sugar attacks) and attend regularly for clinic visits, eye tests and chiropody. People who follow their treatment instructions carefully are less likely to suffer the complications of the disease. You may like to get in touch with Diabetes UK (see p 136).

Diverticulitis

What it is Diverticulitis is a bowel condition causing pain on the left side of the abdomen, with constipation or diarrhoea. It often gives little trouble, but rare complications include infection, abscesses or bowel blockage.

Why it happens Pressure inside the bowel rises because the muscle in the bowel wall is poorly co-ordinated and the diet has little fibre for it to squeeze against. Pockets (diverticula) of lining membrane are forced out and balloon through gaps in the bowel wall. If food debris enters these pockets, it cannot be squeezed out, and may become infected.

How your doctor can help Your doctor will prescribe drugs to relieve painful muscle spasms, or to add fibre to the diet. Antibiotics and surgery may be needed for complications.

Helping yourself Eat a high-fibre diet.

Eye diseases

Cataract

What it is A cataract is the result of change in the protein of the lens of the eye, which gradually becomes cloudy and eventually opaque. (Similar changes occur when egg white is cooked in a frying pan.) The vision of someone with a cataract is at first blurred and colours seem muted, but large, central changes in the lens can blot out part of the field of vision.

Why it happens Cataracts get more common with increasing age. They are also more frequent in people with diabetes, in those who have used steroid medicines and in people who have had an injury to or serious inflammation of the eye. In most cases there is no obvious cause.

How your doctor can help The doctor will refer you to the hospital for a possible 'cataract extraction' in which the cloudy lens is taken out. It is replaced by a substitute lens, either within the eye (a lens implant) or in contact lenses or spectacles.

Helping yourself While waiting for the operation, avoid the glare of bright light, which will further cloud your vision. A wide-brimmed hat or an eyeshade will help outdoors on sunny days, and lamps at home should have shades to diffuse over-bright light.

Plan for your care after the operation. You will usually be advised to avoid bending forwards or getting the area wet, so it is wise to wash your hair before the operation. You will need eye drops for a time after the operation. The hospital staff or the district nurse will show you how to use these; if you still have difficulty, 'Autodrop' or other devices from the pharmacy may make you better able to manage on your own.

Conjunctivitis ('pink eye')

What it is The conjunctiva, the thin membrane that lines the eyelids and covers part of the eyeball, becomes red and inflamed, and the eye feels gritty and sore, discharging pus or clear fluid.

Why it happens The conjunctiva becomes infected by bacteria or viruses. Conjunctivitis can also be an allergic reaction, when the red eye is itchy.

How your doctor can help The doctor will help by prescribing antibiotic drops for infections and advising on general hygiene. Drugs can also reduce the allergic response and relieve its symptoms.

Helping yourself You should see the doctor. Conjunctivitis is usually easily treated and not at all serious, but some other causes of a red eye can be more dangerous.

Diabetes and the eye

What happens The blood vessels of the retina, the thin film at the back of the eye, bulge and leak, causing damage and gradual loss of sight. This is called *background retinopathy*. In other cases new, weak blood vessels form;

this is called *proliferative retinopathy*. They can rupture, sometimes detaching the retina and producing sudden sight loss.

Why it happens The longer a person has diabetes and the worse it is controlled, the more likely these problems are to happen.

How your doctor can help Your doctor will help by supporting your efforts to follow your treatment, with help from hospital doctors, dietitians and nurses when needed. There may be a diabetic clinic at the surgery. The condition proliferative retinopathy, which affects the retina, may require specialist laser treatment.

Helping yourself Keep your diabetes well controlled by attending the diabetic clinic regularly. To keep your sight as good as possible, you should go for regular eye checks and for laser treatment as necessary.

Note People with diabetes are more likely than others to develop cataracts or glaucoma, and these are managed in the usual way.

Giant cell arteritis

What it is This is a condition in which sufferers feel generally unwell, with a bad headache, tender scalp and blurred or incomplete vision.

Why it happens The arteries of the face, scalp and eye become inflamed and partially blocked by giant cells, so the tissues they supply receive insufficient blood for their needs.

How your doctor can help The doctor is likely to send you at once to a hospital eye department. There the diagnosis suggested by the symptoms can be established by a blood test and by biopsy of a scalp artery to look for the tell-tale inflammation and giant cells. Steroid treatment will control the symptoms and prevent deterioration of your sight.

Helping yourself If you lose the whole or part of the sight of one eye, do not delay, but seek medical advice at once.

Glaucoma

What it is Glaucoma is an illness in which the retina is damaged by a rise in pressure of the fluids inside the eye. A person who develops this condition gradually loses their peripheral sight – what is visible round the edges of whatever you are looking at. Without treatment, this eventually causes 'tunnel vision', which is similar to limiting what you can see by looking down a tube. Glaucoma usually develops gradually without the person knowing anything is wrong. It is diagnosed by measuring the pressure inside eye, and once this has been done treatment can prevent further worsening of sight. A few patients have acute attacks of glaucoma, when the pressure rises suddenly. This causes sickness, pain and redness of the eye, and loss of vision. Urgent treatment is needed, usually surgery.

Why it happens The fluid that carries oxygen and nourishment to the inside of the eyeball fails to drain out again properly and builds up inside it, causing pressure damage to the retina.

How your doctor can help The doctor will prescribe tablets or eye drops to slow down the production of fluid and to help it to drain away. If necessary, you can be referred to the hospital for surgery.

Helping yourself Have an eye test at least every two years; this can detect the changes of glaucoma early enough to prevent further damage and loss of sight. If you have some sight loss, you may want to read the suggestions in the section 'Making the most of remaining sight' (p 62).

Macular degeneration

What it is Macular degeneration (sometimes called ageing maculopathy) is another common cause of sight loss in later life. The person affected notices progressive difficulty with tasks requiring close vision and fine discrimination, such as reading small print or recognising faces. There may seem to be a black or blurred patch in the middle of the field of vision which 'gets in the way', and, because the retina is no longer flat, straight lines may seem wavy. Peripheral vision is unimpaired, so people with this condition are still able to find their way about independently.

Why it happens The central, most sensitive, part of the retina becomes patchily detached from the blood vessels behind it, and the separated parts die for lack of blood. The underlying cause is unclear.

How your doctor can help A few cases are helped by laser treatment, and the doctor can refer you for this if it is likely to help.

Helping yourself See 'Making the most of remaining sight', below.

Retinal detachment

What it is The thin, fragile retina separates from its backing, loses its blood supply and dies.

Why it happens The retina can be jolted loose by a blow to the head, or pulled away by the shrinking clot formed after blood has leaked from a blood vessel. This is especially common in people with diabetes.

How your doctor can help Your doctor can refer you promptly to an eye hospital. If the diagnosis is made in time, a laser beam can be used to stick down the edges of the tear before it extends, to prevent any further loss of vision. Once an appreciable amount of retina has stripped away, an open operation is required.

Helping yourself When a retina is stretched and about to tear, its owner sees flashing lights. If you experience this, or if you lose the whole or part of the sight of an eye, you should report to the doctor or hospital without delay.

Making the most of remaining sight

- Do not accept deteriorating vision as an incurable consequence of increasing age, but get the cause diagnosed.
- Consider becoming registered as partially sighted or blind, as this will entitle you to extra services such as the loan of low vision aids from the hospital eye service. Ask to be referred to the ophthalmologist (eye specialist) at the hospital for this to be done.
- Ask your local social services department for an assessment visit from the social worker for visually handicapped people.
- Contact the Royal National Institute for the Blind (RNIB) for further information about equipment and services that might help you.
- Listen to BBC Radio 4's *In Touch* programme, for topical information. You may also be interested in some of their publications.

Falls

What they are Falls are understandably feared by older people, because of their medical and social consequences. A fracture of the hip is sometimes fatal, because of complications, and in other cases leads to a loss of independence and perhaps a move away from a much-loved home. A blow to the head can result in a slow-growing blood clot (subdural haematoma), which causes confusion and other nervous system signs before ending in unconsciousness and death. Lying on the floor unable to get up is not only distressing; it can also lead to hypothermia (being very cold), pneumonia and pressure sores, which may be a serious threat to health. Even bruising in an older person can be painful enough to cause distress and restrict activity for several weeks. It is not surprising, therefore, that an older person who has had a fall may lose their confidence and 'go off their legs' for fear of another fall. This is sad because, falls notwithstanding, there is no doubt that keeping active when older improves the quality of life.

Why they happen Falls may be 'trips' or 'turns', though it is worth remembering that several factors from both groups may interact to result in a fall. Trips are common among younger retired people, sometimes because of unwise risk taking, like standing precariously on furniture to hang curtains or change a light bulb. Other trip hazards include little mats and rugs, torn or rucked-up carpets, trailing flexes, footstools, doorstops, raised thresholds and uneven paving in gardens. (The prevention of trips is discussed in the section on home safety, on pp 111–112.)

Turns are more complex. As we get older, the 'righting reflexes' that steady us and stop us falling when we lose our balance seem to work more slowly. If we cannot regain our balance quickly, we will hit the ground. It is important not to over-estimate the effects of ageing on stability, however; exercise sessions that strengthen muscles and practise balance have been found to reduce the risks of falls even in very old, frail people.

Almost any illness can make an older person unsteady on their feet. Falls can also be caused by anything that reduces the amount of blood reaching the brain; a common example of this is postural hypotension – an exaggeration of the fall in blood pressure on standing up. This can be aggravated by conditions such as Parkinson's disease and diabetes. It may also be worsened by medicines such as sleeping tablets, tranquillisers and drugs for high blood pressure, though it is sometimes difficult to decide whether the benefits of stopping a drug of this sort outweigh the risks. Alcohol may contribute to unsteadiness, either on its own or by interacting with medicines.

Poor heart function can reduce the brain's blood supply and thus cause falls. Disturbance of the heart's normal rhythm (cardiac arrhythmia) is especially likely to do this. Arthritis of the neck vertebrae may reduce blood supply by squashing the blood vessels that run within them, and also interfere with the transmission to the brain of information about the position of the head in space, needed for the efficient operation of the 'righting reflexes'.

How your doctor can help Your doctor can identify and, if possible, treat illnesses that cause falls, while improving your general health and altering drug therapy if this will help. In doing this, it will help to get a good account of the falls from you and from anyone else who witnessed them. A careful examination and appropriate tests should follow. All this should happen before you and anyone around you have lost confidence in your independence.

Helping yourself If you have fallen, do not be fobbed off with suggestions that your troubles are due to 'age' and that 'nothing can be done'. If necessary, ask to be referred to the geriatric department at the local hospital. Once under investigation, you may be asked to keep a 'falls diary'. In this you note the circumstances of any fall:

- what you were doing at the time;
- where you were;
- what time of day it was; and
- whether you had noticed anything unusual about your health beforehand.

A pattern in the falls diary may help identify a likely cause: for instance, falls that happen in the same place might suggest that a particular trip hazard is responsible.

Good investigation and treatment may make it possible to banish your falls completely. If, however, this cannot be done, you may want to consider ways of making yourself much safer, such as getting rid of dangerously hard and sharp objects (eg fenders) that you could fall on. An alarm by which you can call for help – for example, one worn on your wrist or as a pendant – can eliminate the risk of being left for a long period of time. Finally, it is important to remember that under-activity and over-protection by other well-meaning people also have their dangers. The price of safety is too high if it is achieved at the expense of quality of life.

Flu

What it is True influenza is more serious than a cold. The sick person has a high temperature, and the fever is accompanied by severe muscle pains and a bad headache. People with flu cannot go about their usual daily routine, and may become very unwell. A period of depression is quite common in convalescence.

Why it happens Flu is a viral illness, which tends to occur in epidemics. Fortunately, the approaching viruses can usually be identified each autumn, and a tailor-made vaccine prepared against them.

How your doctor can help Your doctor will watch for complications such as chest infections, treating them with antibiotics if they occur. Flu vaccinations will prevent attacks.

Helping yourself If you suffer from diabetes or heart, lung or kidney disease, you should certainly have an annual flu vaccination; it is now being suggested that all people over 65 should do this as well.

If you get flu, pain relief, fluids and general care will help. You are likely to feel worse for longer than with a cold, so may need extra help from family, friends or other carers.

Haemorrhoids

What they are Often called 'piles', these happen when the lining of the back passage slips down, swells and bleeds. The bright red blood stains the toilet paper after a stool (bowel movement) is passed, and between stools the piles hurt and itch.

Why they happen Piles in women may start during pregnancy from the pressure of the baby's head on pelvic veins. Piles seem to be more common in both men and women if their diet lacks dietary fibre and they become constipated.

How the doctor can help Having examined you to make sure that piles and nothing more serious are the cause of the trouble, the doctor can prescribe creams or suppositories to make you more comfortable. Occasionally, surgical treatment is advisable.

Helping yourself Preventing constipation will reduce symptoms. Blood from the back passage should always be reported to the doctor; on occasions it can be a sign of a bowel cancer (see p 50), and this is curable when treated promptly.

Heart attack
(coronary thrombosis or myocardial infarction)

What it is Because the coronary arteries supplying the heart are 'furred up' by fatty atheromatous deposits, the heart muscle does not get sufficient oxygen-rich blood for its needs and is damaged. In middle-aged people this usually causes severe, crushing chest pain, often spreading to the arms and neck; older people may have little or no pain, but may faint, fall, vomit or become breathless or confused.

Why it happens A 'furred' coronary artery blocks completely, so the part of the heart muscle it should supply dies for want of blood. Older people from the Indian sub-continent are especially likely to have heart attacks.

How your doctor can help You will probably need to go into hospital for treatment. This may involve aspirin and other 'clot-busting' drugs to disperse blockages or correcting complications such as heart failure or faulty heart rhythm with drugs or a pacemaker. Surgical treatment can also be used: angioplasty involves stretching a narrowed coronary artery, while in coronary artery bypass grafting (CABG) a new length of vessel is put in, to divert blood round a blocked or badly narrowed section of coronary artery.

Helping yourself Lifestyle changes as for angina reduce the chances of a second heart attack. A positive outlook and a graded return to activity reduce long-term disability, and a supervised exercise programme may help with this.

If you think you are at risk of a heart attack, discuss with your doctor the possibility of taking regular aspirin.

Heart failure

What it is Heart failure happens when the heart cannot provide adequate blood circulation. The person becomes breathless and develops a bluish colour around the lips. If the person is up and about, their ankles will swell due to retained fluid; if confined to bed, the fluid will settle at the lowest point and cause swelling at the base of the spine.

Why it happens It comes about when the heart muscle has been weakened by a heart attack or strained by high blood pressure. A chest infection can make it worse.

How your doctor can help If you or someone you are caring for seems to have heart failure, the ill person should see the doctor urgently. If the diagnosis is confirmed, the doctor will prescribe appropriate drugs. Angiotensin-converting enzyme (ACE) inhibitors relieve the symptoms and improve the amount of exercise that can be taken as well as reducing the likelihood of relapses. Diuretics will help to get rid of the extra fluid that causes the swelling. Digoxin may be added if the ACE inhibitor is poorly tolerated or is ineffective on its own.

Helping yourself Your doctor will probably suggest a low-salt diet, and you should follow this. Regular exercise within the limits of what you can do comfortably will improve the function of your heart and help to keep you independent. Make sure you have vaccinations each autumn to protect you against flu and pneumonia, and try to avoid taking the non-steroidal anti-inflammatory drugs such as ibuprofen and diclofenac, as these can cause fluid retention.

Heart rhythm disorders
(cardiac arrhythmias)

What they are The heart beats irregularly, so you may experience palpitations (an uncomfortable awareness of the heartbeat) or may notice nothing abnormal. More serious abnormalities can cause breathlessness, falls or attacks of unconsciousness. Rhythm disturbances can be of all grades of severity, from harmless to rapidly fatal.

Why they happen Many cases come about because the heart muscle is getting insufficient blood for its needs, and some serious cases follow a heart attack. Other causes include thyroid gland disease, unwanted effects of medicines and too much coffee or tea.

How your doctor can help Your doctor will arrange for an electrocardiogram (ECG) to identify the type of rhythm disturbance. You may be asked to wear a recording machine for 24 hours to monitor your heart for a longer period than for the standard tracing. You may be referred to the cardiologist (heart specialist) for further advice. Treatment may involve medicines such as digoxin, to steady the heart beat, or warfarin, to lessen the risk of clots forming and causing complications such as stroke. Alternatively, a pacemaker may be used. This is a simple electrical device consisting of a battery with a wire to conduct an electrical impulse to the heart and so stimulate it to beat. The pattern of stimulation can be programmed to its wearer's needs by incorporating a microchip. Pacemakers sometimes save lives, but more often they improve quality of life by preventing faintness, breathlessness and falls.

Helping yourself Take your medicines exactly as directed, and ask your doctor if you should change your lifestyle in any way. Pacemakers (see above) usually work well, but if yours malfunctions you should go to the pacemaker clinic as soon as possible. If you have attacks of unconsciousness you should not drive a car.

Hernias

A hernia happens when part of the gut slips into the wrong position. Two types of hernia are common in older people: inguinal hernia and hiatus hernia; femoral hernia is less common.

Inguinal hernia

What it is Commonly called a rupture, this happens when part of the bowel slips out of the abdominal cavity into the scrotum in a man or the labium (hairy area of the genitals) in a woman, forming a swelling that becomes larger as the day goes on. It can often be pushed back into the abdomen if the person lies down. If it gets stuck ('irreducible'), the bowel loop may be 'strangulated' and lose its blood supply, becoming tense and tender. Abdominal pain and vomiting result, and urgent surgery is needed.

How your doctor can help Your doctor will usually refer you for an operation. This replaces the slipped bowel in the abdominal cavity and keeps it there by permanently blocking its exit route. A truss to block the hernia's 'way out' by external pressure will be prescribed only if you are unable or unwilling to undergo surgery.

Helping yourself Hernias are less common in non-smokers, people of normal weight and those with firm abdominal muscles, so preventing hernia may be yet another benefit of changing your lifestyle. If you wear a truss, find out how to put it on properly; do so in bed before getting up and keep it on all day.

Femoral hernia

What it is This is a small swelling in the groin, formed by a loop of bowel from within the abdominal cavity. This is the most common hernia to become 'strangulated', so a femoral hernia is always treated surgically.

Hiatus hernia

What it is This happens when part of the stomach slips up through the diaphragm into the chest. This may cause pain if stomach acid flows back up to irritate the gullet, and the sore area may bleed, causing anaemia.

How your doctor can help Your doctor will prescribe drugs to reduce the amount of acid secreted, or to coat the gullet lining and protect it from attack.

Helping yourself Try sleeping with the head of the bed raised, lose excess weight and avoid bending after meals, which squeezes stomach acid up into the gullet.

High blood pressure
(hypertension, high BP)

What it is We all need the pressure of the heart's squeezing action to keep the blood flowing round the body. However, people with higher than normal blood pressure are more likely than others to suffer from heart attack, stroke or failing kidneys. These risks are reduced if the blood pressure is lowered. High blood pressure usually does not cause any particular symptoms, so blood pressure measurement is necessary to find out whether it is high.

Why it happens Usually no particular cause is found, though tests will be done to identify the few cases that are linked to other illnesses. Lifestyle factors may be important; these include smoking, excess alcohol, too much salt in the diet, overweight, lack of exercise and poor stress management. Older people from the Afro-Caribbean community are especially likely to have high blood pressure.

How your doctor can help Having identified the problem, the doctor can order investigations and prescribe drug treatment, lifestyle changes or both. Check-ups will establish whether this is working properly and find a treatment with the minimum unwanted effects.

Helping yourself Make sure your blood pressure is checked every year; if it is found to be high, attend for check-ups as often as your doctor suggests. Adopt a healthy lifestyle (see pp 1–11), and, if medicines are prescribed for you, take them regularly as prescribed.

Incontinence

What it is Incontinence is the leakage of urine or stool (faeces) at the wrong time or in the wrong place.

Why it happens There are many causes, and often several factors interact. Ageing changes do not cause incontinence in themselves, but may mean that less has to go wrong before it happens. Common causes of urinary incontinence include:

■ urinary infections, when the urine has a foul, often fishy, smell;
■ weakness of the pelvic floor muscles following childbirth, made worse

by lack of oestrogen after the menopause; this leads to stress incontinence (leakage when the woman laughs or coughs);

- prostate gland enlargement, which can cause dribbling incontinence;
- stroke and other diseases of the nervous system, which can interfere
  with control of the bladder;
- the unwanted effects of medicines; common culprits include diuretics
  (which cause an increased flow of urine and over-load the system) and
  sedative medicines (which reduce awareness of bladder filling and
  slow down progress to the lavatory);
- constipation (see p 53);
- uncontrolled diabetes, when the extra sugar in the body acts like a
  diuretic;
- poor mobility, delaying reaching the lavatory, and poor finger dexterity
  in coping with clothing when there;
- loss of the ability to plan visits to the lavatory in someone with dementia;
- increased irritability of the bladder in anxiety, and slowness and loss of
  motivation in people with a depressive illness.

How your doctor can help Doctors can look for 'medical' causes such
as those above, and treat them appropriately. They can also refer you to
other helpful professionals, such as the continence adviser, who can show
you how to do pelvic floor exercises, which are helpful in cases of stress
incontinence, and other useful behavioural techniques. The continence
adviser can also give advice about the best pads and pants to use to minimise embarrassment, if these are necessary.

Helping yourself An occupational therapist (OT) may be able to recommend equipment that will make the lavatory easier to use, such as grab
rails or a raised toilet seat. The OT can be reached through the social services department. If there is a long wait for a visit, you may like to consider
buying what you need at a Disabled Living Centre or by mail order. Boots
the Chemist have a catalogue for telephone or mail order, or you can look
in your *Yellow Pages* under 'Disabled Equipment'. You might also like to send
for Age Concern's Factsheet 42 *Disability equipment and how to get it*.

Try to make sure that you drink enough fluid in every 24 hours: 1.5–2
litres (3–5 pints); you can space your drinks so that visits to the lavatory
come at convenient times, provided the full amount is taken over each 24-
hour period. Drinking less can lead to dehydration, which can damage the

kidneys and cause confusion. Paradoxically, drinking less can also worsen incontinence, as the concentrated urine can irritate the bladder lining and cause it to empty at the wrong time. For more about incontinence, see pp 112–114.

Osteoporosis

What it is Osteoporosis is thinning and weakening of the bones. It happens to both sexes with increasing age, but is faster and more severe in women after the menopause when levels of female hormones fall. Fractures of the hip and wrist happen more easily in people with osteoporosis, and the vertebrae of the spine can be squashed into wedge shapes by the weight they carry. This causes severe back pain, and results in a stooping posture and loss of height.

How your doctor can help If you are a woman, your doctor can prescribe hormone replacement therapy (HRT) if this is appropriate and you want to take it. Bisphosphonates and calcium treatment also helps to prevent recurrence of fractures in both sexes, and research is trying to identify other suitable bone-strengthening measures for men, or for women as an alternative to HRT.

Helping yourself Women may want to consider discussing HRT with their doctors. A diet containing adequate calcium and vitamin D also helps, and weight-bearing exercise (eg walking) strengthens bones. Smoking and excess alcohol tend to weaken the bones, and should be avoided.

Parkinson's disease

What it is Parkinson's (or PD) is an illness that causes difficulty in moving (bradykinesia), stiffness of muscles (rigidity) and shaking (tremor).

Why it happens The cells of the part of the brain called the basal ganglia die off. They stop producing an important brain chemical (neurotransmitter) called dopamine. The cause is usually unknown, but inherited factors may make it more likely to occur. A few cases of a similar disease are caused by drugs, either 'anti-psychotics' used for some patients with severe mental illness, or some illicit recreational drugs. Parkinson's disease mainly affects older people, but one patient in seven is under 40.

Parkinson's disease threatens independence by slowing the person down and making it more difficult to co-ordinate movement. Starting or stopping an activity is especially difficult, and people affected develop strategies to avoid 'freezing'. They have difficulty walking; they take small, hesitant steps, do not swing their arms, are unsteady and may fall. The limbs feel stiff, and this rigidity makes the person bent and stooped. Poor movement of facial and speech muscles make it difficult to talk, and the voice becomes quieter and more monotonous as the day wears on. There is little change of facial expression, so the person has difficulty in smiling. It is also difficult to swallow saliva, and overflow may lead to drooling. These changes make it difficult to assess the mental state of someone with Parkinson's disease. However, some patients do develop dementia or become depressed.

How your doctor can help Your doctor will refer you to the hospital so you can be prescribed medicines to correct the faults in your brain chemistry. These must be tailored carefully to your needs and then taken strictly as prescribed, never stopping them suddenly. The medicines may need to be readjusted at intervals if you get worse. Treatment from a physiotherapist, occupational therapist or speech therapist may also help you, and you may like to ask your doctor to refer you for this. You or your carer may also want to ask your doctor to arrange for respite or other forms of extra care.

Helping yourself It is especially important to take your medicines strictly according to instructions to get full benefit from them. It will take longer to do tasks yourself than to accept help from others, but doing so will help to keep you as active and independent as possible. You may need to take extra fluids and fibre in your diet to prevent constipation. You and your carers can find out more about your condition from the Parkinson's Disease Society (see p 140).

Peptic ulcer

What it is A peptic ulcer is the result of part of the stomach or duodenal lining being damaged by the acid digestive juices within it. This usually causes pain that is worse when the stomach and duodenum are empty between meals or at night.

Why it happens The cause is not fully understood, though infection with the bacterium *Helicobacter pylori* may be responsible. Smoking, excess coffee and alcohol, and the non-steroidal anti-inflammatory (NSAI) drugs used for arthritis tend to worsen symptoms.

How the doctor can help Your doctor can order tests to make sure that the ulcer is benign (not cancerous). The gut lining can be inspected directly through a gastroscope or duodenoscope, or a barium meal (which will outline the ulcer on X-ray) can be ordered. The ulcer can usually be healed by tablets or medicines designed to reduce acid secretion, and it may be helpful to eliminate the *H pylori*. Surgery is rarely needed nowadays except for complications such as severe bleeding or perforation, when the ulcer eats right through the gut wall.

Helping yourself It will help to stop smoking and to avoid excess alcohol and any foods that seem to upset you.

Prostate gland enlargement

What it is This is the growth in size of the chestnut-shaped gland that lies at the base of the bladder and contributes fluid to the semen. The tube (urethra) that carries urine from the bladder to the outside runs through the prostate, and enlargement of the gland interferes with the free passage of urine. Affected men have a poor urinary stream, with difficulty in starting to pass urine and dribbling as they finish. This leakage can stain clothes and bed-linen and cause smell. Because of the partial blockage, the bladder becomes unable to empty itself completely, so the person affected feels the need to pass water frequently both day and night. A stagnant pool of urine accumulates, which may become infected and thus make the incontinence worse. Eventually the man may become unable to pass urine at all, and needs admission to hospital for this 'retention of urine' to be relieved. Meanwhile, the dammed-up urine can cause serious kidney damage from the pressure and infection.

Why it happens The cause of the enlargement is not really understood, though male hormones such as testosterone are known to stimulate prostatic growth.

How your doctor can help The doctor may suggest blood tests and/or a biopsy to make sure the prostate is not cancerous (see p 51). Drugs to shrink the gland a little may help your symptoms. You may be referred to a surgeon at the hospital for an operation to remove part of the gland. This is often done through an instrument passed up the penis through the urethra (transurethral resection or TUR), but sometimes an operation (open prostatectomy) through an incision in the abdominal wall is necessary. A catheter is left in place to drain urine for the first few days until bleeding stops, after which it is removed and urine can be passed normally again. The TUR does not usually cause impotence, but may cause retrograde ejaculation – at orgasm the semen does not squirt out of the end of the penis but flows into the bladder. It is then passed with the urine, which becomes cloudy. The open prostatectomy may cause impotence, so you should discuss this risk with the surgeon if the operation is suggested to you.

Helping yourself It is wise to visit the doctor so that he or she can make sure the growth is not cancerous (see p 48). If you are prescribed medicines, take them as prescribed. They may affect sexual function; if this concerns you, report it to the doctor. If you are waiting for a prostate operation, drink most of your fluids in the daytime to avoid having to get up to the lavatory too often at night. However, make sure that you do not become dehydrated, as this can damage your kidneys.

Stoma

What it is A stoma is an opening made by surgery on the abdominal wall through which the bowel contents drain into a bag rather than being passed into the lavatory. A *colostomy* has the large intestine or colon opening on the abdominal wall, and is the likeliest stoma for an older person to have; an *ileostomy* comes from higher up the bowel, and a *urostomy* is a loop of bowel that collects and drains urine, acting as a substitute for the bladder. Some stomas are temporary, to rest the bowel, and are soon closed, but some are permanent.

Why they are formed A colostomy may be necessary when a large part of the bowel has to be cut out because of a cancer or other bowel disease.

How your doctor can help Your doctor can help by arranging for you to meet someone who already copes with a stoma, before your operation. Afterwards the doctor can prescribe medicines to stabilise its function, and make sure that any medicines you take for other conditions will suit you despite your stoma.

Helping yourself Make sure you know how to get in touch with your local stoma nurse for advice on leading an enjoyable life despite your stoma. You may also find it helpful to contact the British Colostomy Association (for address, see p 133).

Stroke

What it is A stroke (also called cerebrovascular accident or CVA) happens when a brain artery is blocked or bursts. Blockage prevents part of the brain from getting the blood it needs, and the affected part of the brain cannot work properly any more. Sometimes the blockage clears itself before the brain is damaged, so the signs of the stroke then go away; this is called a *transient ischaemic attack* (TIA). Persisting blockage causes permanent brain damage from lack of blood, and this is called *cerebral infarction*. Most strokes in older people (85 per cent) are due either to slow blockage by a clot (thrombosis) or to rapid blockage by a piece of detached atheroma that gets stuck (embolism).

When a brain blood vessel bursts, blood gushes out and the expanding clot squashes the brain; this is called a *cerebral haemorrhage*. A rapid and severe episode with a large amount of blood can squash the brain so much that it causes coma and death; in less severe cases the person may survive with variable amounts of brain damage.

After a stroke, the part of the body controlled by the dead area of brain cannot work properly any more, so the effect on a person depends on which part of the brain has been put out of action. One common pattern is of weakness and loss of feeling down one side of the body, and speech and vision may also be affected. Another group of people who have had a stroke have difficulty in swallowing and choke easily.

Why it happens Sticky blood in 'furred' pipes makes blockage strokes more likely, whether the furring narrows the artery or breaks off to form emboli. Strokes are therefore more common in people with high blood pressure, diabetes and blood disorders, especially if they smoke, do not take exercise or eat a high-fat diet. Bursts are more common in people with bulging weak points, called aneurysms, on their brain arteries, especially if they have high blood pressure or impaired blood clotting. Some people are born with aneurysms, and others seem to acquire them during life as a result of an unhealthy lifestyle. Afro-Caribbean people are especially likely to have strokes because of high blood pressure. People from the Indian sub-continent are also vulnerable to stroke, although the reason is less clear.

How your doctor can help The doctor will help by making the diagnosis, by organising rehabilitation and sometimes by treatment to prevent recurrence. Unfortunately, there is no treatment yet to reduce the brain damage or put it right, though much research is being done.

Helping yourself A healthy lifestyle makes a stroke less likely to happen. After a stroke, working on rehabilitation improves function, and this is really worthwhile. Your family and friends can give you moral support and encourage you to do as much as possible for yourself.

The Stroke Association keeps a database of Stroke Clubs around the country and also stocks useful and reasonably priced literature for people who have had a stroke and their carers (for the address, see p 144).

The thyroid gland

What it is This gland is U-shaped, lies at the base of the neck and is responsible for energy release in most body tissues and organs. Its commonest problems are under-activity, over-activity and growths (goitre).

Why disorders happen The cause of problems is usually not known, though under-activity can follow thyroid surgery.

What they are like Thyroid under-activity (hypothyroidism or myxoedema) causes weight gain, sluggishness and mental dullness; it also makes the person more vulnerable to hypothermia (low body temperature). Over-activity (thyrotoxicosis) is a cause of heart problems, especially rhythm disturbances, most commonly in older women. It also causes weight loss and generally poor health. In older people the commonest sort of growths are nodules of hardened but otherwise normal thyroid tissue; very few are cancerous.

How your doctor can help Your doctor will probably do some tests and then refer you to a hospital specialist. Under-activity is treated by replacing the missing hormone; the dose will be tailored to your particular needs, and will be continued for life. Over-activity can be treated in one or more of three ways: using radioactive iodine to switch off the thyroid cells, drug treatment or surgery.

Helping yourself Get to know your body's workings, and seek help from the doctor if you notice a persistent change in functioning, especially unexplained loss of weight. If you are prescribed thyroid hormone replacement, be very careful to take it as prescribed and not to run out of tablets.

Tinnitus

What it is Tinnitus is noises in the ear, which are often most troublesome at night. Many, but not all, people with tinnitus are also deaf.

Why it happens The cause is usually a malfunction of the nervous tissue of the inner ear. Occasionally it happens as a toxic effect of medicines; only very rarely is it a sign of illness.

How your doctor can help Your doctor and colleagues in the ENT (ear, nose and throat) department of the hospital can examine you and usually will be able to reassure you that nothing serious is wrong. In severe cases a tinnitus masker may be suggested; this device fits behind the ear like a conventional hearing aid and produces a noise that conceals the tinnitus. This needs to be fitted by an expert and is unfortunately not nationally available on the NHS.

Helping yourself Once you are no longer worried about the cause, you may find that you are able to ignore the tinnitus as you would a ticking clock. Others use a radio or personal stereo to drown out the noise. The British Tinnitus Association provides information, funds research and runs self-help groups, and you may want to consider getting in touch with them (for the address, see p 134).

Varicose veins and ulcers

What they are These are veins that are stretched and more winding than normal. The pocket-like valves that normally prevent backward flow of blood can no longer work properly, so the veins become even more stretched and out of shape. People with varicose veins complain of aching and swollen legs, as well as the unsightly appearance. The veins may become inflamed (phlebitis) and may bleed profusely if injured. The tissues that are poorly drained by the veins may break down to form a varicose ulcer, usually on the inside of the leg just above the ankle, and this may be surrounded by an area of itching skin – varicose eczema.

Why they happen A tendency to develop them may run in families; this is worsened by prolonged standing or being overweight.

How your doctor can help Surgery is sometimes recommended; the veins may be removed completely or injected with a substance that will clot and shrink them. More often, elastic stockings will be prescribed; you should put them on in bed, while the veins are empty. The usual treatment for varicose ulcers is pressure bandaging by the district or practice nurse; occasionally a skin graft is needed to complete healing. If you develop a varicose ulcer and it does not heal within three months, ask your GP to refer you to an ulcer specialist.

Helping yourself Try to avoid spending long periods standing up, and when sitting, raise your feet above the level of your bottom to help fluid drainage. Walking usually helps to disperse fluid, and is therefore helpful.

Complementary or alternative medicine

People have every right to decide whether to use complementary or traditional medicine, as well as or instead of orthodox, scientific Western medicine. Beliefs about health and illness vary a great deal, especially in people from different cultural backgrounds. One common pattern would be to use traditional remedies for chronic (long-term), vague disorders, and orthodox Western medicine for acute (short-term) illness or injuries.

In general, complementary therapies that genuinely have good effects can in certain circumstances be actively harmful, while those that do little good also do little harm. However, in serious illness either may delay the use of effective treatment, so precious time in producing a cure is lost.

Herbal remedies

Many of the drugs now available in the chemists' shop/pharmacy were originally extracted from plants. For example, digitalis (digoxin) came from foxgloves, aspirin from willow bark and colchicine from the autumn crocus.

Western herbal medicines can be obtained from a herbalist or bought over the counter in a health food shop. Herbal medicines are common in Chinese medicine, and are often used in cases of eczema. However, some preparations have been found to contain steroids, so it is difficult to know how effective the herbs alone might be. Unwanted effects from herbal treatments are quite common and may be serious or, rarely, fatal. They include kidney and liver damage, with reports of liver cancer, blood disorders and skin rashes. People often think that, because herbal remedies are 'natural', they must be safe. Unfortunately, this is not the case and, just as Western medicines can have unwanted effects, so can herbal remedies.

Western medicines and herbal medicines may interact in a person who uses both, so do be sure to tell your doctor or pharmacist if you are using herbal remedies.

Homoeopathy

Homoeopathic medicine is based on a number of principles. One is that 'like cures like': giving a small quantity of a substance that causes the symptoms helps the body to fight the disease. Another is that the minimal dose has the greatest effect: homoeopathic medicines are always prepared in a very diluted form. They are unlikely, therefore, either to relieve symptoms or produce unwanted effects. However, as they might delay effective treatment, it is probably best to consult a qualified doctor who also practises homoeopathy.

Osteopathy and chiropractic

These seem to be genuinely helpful in some bone and joint conditions. They are among the most widely used of the complementary therapies, and many orthodox doctors recommend them to their patients.

Just as these forms of 'manipulative medicine' can be useful, they can also have unwanted effects. Manipulation can damage bones, joints and nearby tissues such as nerves. This can usually be prevented if the medical diagnosis is made before manipulative treatment is attempted, and good osteopaths and chiropractors usually make sure this is done.

Chiropractic is now regulated by the statutory body the General Chiropractic Council.

Acupuncture and shiatsu

Acupuncture is a Chinese therapy in which fine needles are inserted into the body at points corresponding to organs of the body in Chinese traditional medicine. In shiatsu, the principles are the same, but finger pressure is applied to the acupuncture points, rather than needles. The techniques are said to work by releasing the body's natural pain-killers, the endorphins. Research suggests that these techniques may help in a small proportion of cases, but the effects are not consistent.

It is important that acupuncture needles are properly sterilised between patients, as otherwise hepatitis B, HIV or other infections may be transferred from one person to another.

Traditional Asian medicines

'Hakims' or traditional healers give advice and provide medicines in the Muslim community. These medicines may contain toxic amounts of metals such as arsenic and mercury, and this has sometimes caused serious disability through nerve damage. Sadly, some users have even died.

Faith healing

Reputable faith healers try to supply spiritual support to add to what orthodox medicine can provide. They will encourage the sick person to see a doctor to obtain a diagnosis, and will not contradict orthodox medical advice. This is important, because stopping medical treatment (tablets for epilepsy, for instance) after an apparent healing can have serious or even fatal results.

Some people who are not healed come to blame themselves for their lack of faith. They start to think that their illness is all their own fault, and develop a crippling sense of guilt.

Many people have long-standing conditions that fluctuate mysteriously from time to time. Arthritis, irritable bowel syndrome and eczema are examples of ailments that seem to be affected by physical factors such as the person's diet and workload, chemicals they are in contact with, changes in the weather and the person's mental state at the time. Whenever someone gets better, it is easy to decide that the improvement is due to whichever treatment – orthodox or complementary – is in use at the time, whatever other factor might be responsible.

Another important influence is the 'placebo effect': in about a third of cases, something a person believes to be effective will help their symptoms, even if it (the placebo) has no active ingredients. Placebos have their snags, however: the good effect does not always happen, and, if it does, it does not last for long. Also, once the 'medicine' has apparently been effective, the person is likely to resist any suggestion that psychological treatment might be helpful, even when this might be so. In any case, many doctors are reluctant to use placebos, because they think it is paternalistic and insulting to deceive their patients.

Orthodox medicines have powerful benefits, but can also cause serious unwanted effects. Because of this, they undergo searching scientific tests before they can be used. Many people would like to see complementary medicines tested in the same way; this would mean that useful ones could be used with confidence, and useless or dangerous ones abandoned.

The Older Carer

More than a million carers are over retirement age, perhaps looking after a partner, a sibling or a parent. Many took on their responsibilities willingly and cheerfully, though some find that, as they get older themselves, keeping going is more difficult. This chapter suggests some ways of easing the task a little. Support for carers is not generous, and in some parts of the country is sparse; even so, well-informed carers who know what they need and ask for it assertively are the most likely to succeed in getting help. (For simplicity, we refer to the person you are caring for as 'your relative').

Points to remember

- As a carer, you have a right to help; it is not 'charity'.
- Everyone has their own needs, and carers are no exception; it will not help the person you care for if you break down. Take care of your health and arrange breaks of respite care, so that you have some life of your own.
- Asking for help can be difficult when so much needs to be done. It may help if you start with what you find the most difficult – perhaps coping with incontinence, or a lack of money.
- Though it sounds obvious, it is sensible to try to work out what sort of help you are looking for. After that, do your best to find out the person or agency that is most likely to provide the help you need.
- Make clear requests to the appropriate agency. Do not allow yourself to be side-tracked onto more general issues, but stick to the point.
- Keep a record of your efforts to get help. Note the date of every telephone call and record its content in a short summary. In particular, ask the name of every official you speak to, and write it down.

- Do not give up too easily; in the long run, it will not be easier to manage alone. Polite but dogged persistence seems to be the best way to get help, time after time.

Help with caring

The rest of this chapter is dealt with in alphabetical order:

- aggression
- approaching social services
- benefits
- breaking point
- community alarm systems
- confusion
- dying at home
- equipment to maintain independence or to help with home nursing
- feelings
- general health of your relative
- giving up caring
- home from hospital
- home safety
- incontinence
- living wills
- managing money
- pressure sores
- respite breaks
- risk taking
- support groups
- Wills.

Aggression

This is commonest in people with dementia who have lost the self-control they learned earlier in life. It is especially likely to happen when the person is confronted with their own loss of capabilities, for instance when dressing themselves unaided. Excessive alcohol and some medicines can make things worse. The person may hit out, shout and swear, throw food about or refuse to be washed or cared for in other ways.

Carers are understandably upset by this sort of behaviour, but it may help to remember that the anger is part of the dementing illness. It is not meant personally, and is usually quickly forgotten by the angry person, if not by the carer. With experience, you will discover the sorts of events and circumstances that bring on aggressive behaviour, and can arrange to avoid them as far as possible. Once an attack has started, it is best to separate the angry person from whatever caused the outburst. Do not get too close, or stand over them if they are sitting down, and remember that the angry person may misinterpret your kindly meant arm around their shoulders as an assault. They are usually easily distractible by new circumstances, but if this is not the case, you may want to leave the room, saying 'I will come back when you are calmer'. Try to have a short while alone; you may find a relaxation technique useful as you try to deal with your own anger and upset (see p 28 for a simple one).

When you have a chance to think about the incident, you may be able to spot obvious causes that you can avoid in future. Consider asking for some day care for your relative, or some respite care. A community psychiatric nurse (CPN) may be able to advise you about coping with your relative's difficult behaviour; your doctor's surgery will tell you how to contact one. You may also find it helpful to meet other people who have 'been there', at a carers' group; ask about these at the social services department. Very occasionally your GP or an old age psychiatrist may suggest using medicines to control the behaviour. These are sometimes useful, but the dose has to be very carefully balanced if the person is not to become more difficult to care for.

Eventually it may become clear that your relative can no longer be cared for at home. You may then wish to contact the social services department, which will perform an assessment of your relative's needs (taking your needs into consideration). They may then offer services at home, or agree that residential care is the answer. To find out more about the procedure for getting residential care, read Age Concern's Factsheet 29 Finding residential and nursing home accommodation.

If you as a carer feel driven to retaliate against your relative's aggression, or need to talk about your fears of harming them, you should telephone Action on Elder Abuse, who have an advice helpline (see p 131).

Approaching social services

Social services departments (SSDs) provide access to most non-medical forms of help that a sick, frail or disabled person might need to help them stay at home. This might include someone visiting at home to help with washing and dressing, day care and the transport to reach it, and equipment and adaptations to make the person more independent at home.

You will find the address of your local social services department in the telephone book under the name of your local authority. You should approach them and ask for an assessment. They will need to know the name and address of the person needing care, what is wrong with them (eg multiple sclerosis, Alzheimer's disease) and how this condition interferes with their daily life (eg confines them to a wheelchair, makes them unable to use cooking equipment safely). When your relative is being assessed or re-assessed, you are entitled to be assessed as well concerning your own needs as carer, for instance for a break from caring. Although you can be involved in your relative's assessment, your own assessment can be entirely separate if you so wish. Assessments may not be made at once, and it is sensible to ask the social services department to let you know how long you will have to wait.

After the assessment, a care plan should be made and then shown to you and to the relative or friend you look after. It will outline the suggested pattern of care and explain how the social services department will ensure that it is given as specified. The whole 'package of care' will be reviewed from time to time in case the needs of the person being cared for have changed.

Social services department usually make a charge for the services they provide. For care alone this charge is discretionary, but should be reasonable for the person receiving the care; no one should lack help because they cannot pay for it. Your finances as carer should not be considered, because it is only the person receiving care who is charged. There are national rules for charging for residential or nursing home care.

Perhaps you as carer or the person being cared for are dissatisfied with the amount of care received, the way it is being given (whether direct by the social services department or by someone on their behalf) or the cost of the care. Every social services department is obliged to have a complaints/appeals procedure, and you should ask about this. Make your complaint in writing, with help from the Citizens Advice Bureau or Carers National Association if necessary. Although most complaints will be sorted out at this stage, they can be carried further if necessary, and the Citizens Advice Bureau will help with this.

Benefits

The rules for receiving state benefits can be difficult to understand, but try not to be put off. If you need help in making a claim, the Citizens Advice Bureau or other independent advice centre is a good place to ask. Helpful advice is also available from the local authority's own welfare rights officer and from carers' groups or disability organisations. You may also like to refer to Age Concern's annual publication *Your Rights* or to its Factsheets (see pp 148 and 149).

The following are some short notes on the state benefits that you, or the person you are caring for, are most likely to claim.

Attendance Allowance is payable to a disabled person 65 or over who needs help with personal care, or who is unsafe without someone to watch over them because of a physical or mental illness. It is not means-tested. There are two rates: the lower one is for people who need help either during the day or during the night; the higher one is for people who need help throughout the 24 hours. It is usually necessary for the person concerned to have required care for at least six months prior to the claim before the benefit can be paid, but there are special rules for people who are terminally ill (see the section 'Dying at home', on p 95).

Further information is available in Age Concern's Factsheet 34 *Attendance Allowance and Disability Living Allowance.*

Invalid Care Allowance may be available if you are between 16 and 65 years old, have low earnings and spend 35 hours or more caring for someone who is receiving Attendance Allowance. Claims are made through the Benefits Agency.

Housing Benefit is payable to someone who pays rent or, in almshouses, a weekly maintenance contribution. Eligible people have no more than £16,000 in savings and are on a low income. Anyone who wishes to claim Housing Benefit should apply to the local authority, not to the Benefits Agency. Further information is available in Age Concern's Factsheet 17 *Housing Benefit and Council Tax Benefit*.

Council Tax Benefit is designed to help people with low incomes and no more than £16,000 in savings who have to pay Council Tax. As with Housing Benefit, it is paid through the local authority. Further information is available in Age Concern's Factsheet 17 *Housing Benefit and Council Tax Benefit*.

Retirement Pension seems obvious, but is occasionally overlooked. Eligible people have either paid enough National Insurance contributions or have a spouse who has done so. At the time of writing the pensionable age is 60 for women and 65 for men, but a rise to 65 will be phased in for women born after May 1950.

The Social Fund provides loans and grants and is reached through the Benefits Agency. It provides one-off sums to help people with low incomes to buy expensive items, such as large household appliances or furniture.

Leaflets giving more information about these benefits are available from your local Benefits Agency office (formerly the Department of Social Security office).

Direct payments

These are a way of giving people who need care more control over how their needs are met. Instead of arranging for the services to be provided, the local authority makes payments direct to the person needing care, who then buys in help that is organised as and when they wish – either direct or through a home care agency.

Only people who have been assessed as needing help and who meet the eligibility criteria can receive direct payments. These payments must be used to meet the assessed care needs, not treated as extra income and used for other purposes. But the payments are not taxed and are not taken into account when considering the person's income for Social Security benefits.

Direct payments are gradually being offered by more and more local authorities to more and more people. Originally available only to those under 66, they are coming to be offered to older people as well. This is an enlightened development: direct payments can empower their recipients to control how their care is given, when and by whom, and thus gives them an increased degree of control over their own lives.

Breaking point
Prevention in the long term

- Do not wait until you are desperate – plan for yourself from when you start caring. Allow yourself breaks, take care of your health and give yourself opportunities to have a life of your own.
- Monitor your own distress from day to day; if things are getting worse, take appropriate action to mobilise help.
- If you are finding the tasks of caring increasingly difficult, it is wise to consult your doctor in case your stamina is being undermined by a physical or mental illness such as anaemia or depressive illness.
- Find someone to talk to; many people find carers' groups very useful, there being no substitute for someone who has been through the same experience. There may be one person in the group you find especially easy to talk to and be with. Such a person may be a useful 'telephone buddy', to talk to when things are particularly difficult.
- Some people prefer counselling, when they can express their feelings honestly to someone outside the situation. Counsellors can be found via the GP or through organisations such as Relate and possibly also the Citizens Advice Bureau.

When you find yourself at crisis point

Warning signs include:

- needing pills or alcohol to get through the day;
- contemplating suicide;
- feeling generally unwell, perhaps losing weight progressively;
- shouting or swearing at your relative, or hitting, shaking or otherwise hurting them.

What to do

- Get away from whatever has upset you for a while, even if only by going into the garden or into another room.
- Get rid of physical aggression by punching a pillow. You might also like to call Action on Elder Abuse Response Line (see p 131).
- Settle yourself in a place where you can practise a simple relaxation technique such as the one outlined on page 28.

When you are feeling a bit better, think about ways in which your situation could be improved and try to arrange help that will prevent your becoming so upset again. Organisations that may help include the Carers National Association, Age Concern and the organisation for the condition affecting the person you care for, for instance the Alzheimer's Society (see the 'Useful addresses' section).

Community alarm systems

There are a number of different forms of community alarm systems. When help is required, they may be activated by pressing a button or pulling a cord or in some other way. The call may be answered by someone in a control centre, which may be some distance away, by a mobile warden or, for residents of sheltered housing, by a resident warden. The central control operator may be able to ask a mobile warden to visit the person who has put out the call, or may only be able to pass on a message to a relative, the doctor or an emergency service.

Some older people find that alarm systems give them a feeling of security and boost their confidence. This is particularly so for those with a tendency to fall; with a body-worn trigger for the alarm, they can summon help even if they are unable to get up off the floor. Knowing this often gives them a sufficient boost to morale to increase both their activity and their independence.

On the other hand, few people with a dementing illness can benefit from an alarm. This is because they are unable to recognise an emergency (the suspicious caller, the smoke under the kitchen door) as what it is and call for help. On the other hand, they may make many calls an hour, because they have forgotten they have already made the call or cannot recall what the trigger is for.

There are also alarms with 'inactivity' features; these send out signals if, for instance, the tap is not run or the lavatory not flushed within a certain period of time. Again, these are more helpful with people who are physically disabled than with those who are mentally frail, who might be flooding the kitchen from the running tap or tearing up their money and flushing it away without activating the alarm.

Below are some questions to ask to help you decide whether an alarm system would be useful for your relative.

Is your relative prepared to use an alarm system? Surveys with spot-checks have revealed that large numbers of buttons are placed behind heavy furniture, pull cords are tied up out of reach and body-worn triggers are unworn. If people find the idea of an alarm system unacceptable as an insult to their capabilities or as a depressing reminder that they are not the person they were, there is no point in taking things further.

Is your relative able to use the alarm system? The difficulties of people with dementia have been discussed above, but physical problems are also important. People with arthritic fingers or co-ordination problems may find small controls difficult to manage, hearing-impaired people may not hear quiet voices over an intercom, and people with speech difficulties may need to use a code of signals using bells, buzzers and other noise-makers.

Is an alarm system the best use of the available money? Alarms may be bought by relatives, supplied by local authorities or installed by charities. After installation, there will be running costs and the expense of repairs to consider. The system may be cheap at the price if it gives everyone peace of mind, but will be an expensive mistake if it is unused or misused.

Is your relative's real need for someone to talk to for company, rather than for a lifeline in emergencies? In most cases control centre staff, however kind-hearted, do not have time to spare for chatting. If the person's real need is for social contact, this must be met some other way. Volunteer visitors are sometimes available; they may be adults, but there may also be a 'task force' of boys and girls from local schools. The social services department or the local group/organisation of Age Concern will know about what is available in your area.

A telephone call can be a good second best to a human visitor (Age Concern's Factsheet 28 *Help with telephones* gives information about sources of help with the costs of installing and using a telephone). As well as its social function, the telephone can also be used to check on your relative with a telephone call at a prearranged time. If no answer is obtained, a willing neighbour could be alerted to check that your relative is all right.

Confusion

Confusion is never 'just old age'. There are three possible reasons for confusion: the consequence of physical illness, a form of dementia or a condition that can be mistaken for confusion.

Physical illness

Anyone of any age can become 'delirious' if they are ill enough with a severe infection or some other cause. Older people tend to become confused in this way more easily and when less severely ill than younger people. Someone close to the older person will know that they are 'not themselves', while this may be less obvious to a doctor or nurse who doesn't know them. This sort of confusion usually comes on over a short period of time – often about 24 hours. The person's mental state fluctuates during the day; they are often most rational in the morning and become more confused in the late afternoon and evening. This is the time when they are likely to be most restless and difficult to look after. They commonly see things that are not there, or misinterpret real objects wrongly: for instance, a patterned wallpaper can be 'seen' as crawling with insects. The affected person often has delusions that he or she is threatened or in danger, and this may lead to aggression to carers or attempts to escape from them.

If you are looking after someone who is behaving in this way, it would be wise to call the doctor, explain what is going on and ask for a home visit. Once given appropriate treatment, the person's mental state will slowly return to normal.

A form of dementia

Alzheimer's disease is the commonest sort of dementia, and it starts slowly over a matter of months. People with Alzheimer's disease gradually lose their memory for recent events and do not know where they are, what time it is or the identities of people around them. They are unable to evaluate their surroundings, work out the best course of action and then put it into operation; in other words, they lose their 'if ... then ... so' thinking, such as 'If I hang this tea-towel over the grill, then it could catch fire and become dangerous, so I will put it on the towel rail'. People with dementia lose their former interests: a previously keen gardener may let his allotment become a jungle, and the woman proud of her family loses interest in marriages and births. Loss of inhibitions can be very distressing to relatives and difficult to handle. With learned behaviour patterns lost, the affected person may pass water in the middle of a restaurant or hit the person who pushed in front of them on the escalator, while sexual behaviour can include uninvited groping and open masturbation.

Affected people may try hard to conceal their predicament in any way they can; for instance, they will avoid difficult questions in a mental state examination by 'counter-attacking' with 'if you don't know what day it is, young lady, you shouldn't be doing a job like yours'. Pressing them for a reply often leads to aggression or breakdown into tears – a catastrophe reaction. The mental state of someone with dementia can vary from day to day. An unwary person trying to assess such a person may be deceived by a plausible but quite fictitious account of their abilities, a short-lived mental spurt producing passable test results and the rags of a good social manner.

The next commonest form of dementia is the vascular type, sometimes called multi-infarct dementia. It happens when a series of small strokes lead to the death of progressively more brain. Deterioration happens jerkily, and so, instead of sliding smoothly downhill, the person's mental state goes down in irregular jerks, like an uneven flight of steps. This is most likely to happen in someone who has other vascular problems, causing angina, major strokes or circulation problems in the legs. Someone with vascular dementia has difficulties similar to someone with Alzheimer's disease.

Although at the moment there is no cure for dementia, it is sensible to get the diagnosis made if possible, as new drugs can slow progression of the disease in some people. Also, a diagnosis of dementia may improve access to services. There is no simple test to give an answer in the early stages but, as time passes and the person is observed, the probable dementia may become a virtual certainty. Many different forms of help are available, including day centres, respite care and carers who come to the home to provide personal care or advise on coping with behaviour difficulties. You might also find it helpful to read Age Concern's book *Caring for someone who has dementia* by Jane Brotchie, or to approach the Alzheimer's Society (address on p 131) for some of their useful literature.

A condition that can be mistaken for confusion

Mistaking another condition for confusion is especially likely to happen with people who do not know the older person very well, such as nursing staff in hospital or care staff in a day centre. Poor sight and hearing can make a person seem confused even when they are not, and so can the effects of a severe upset such as a bereavement or moving out of the family home into sheltered housing or residential care. It will help if you explain about your relative's sight or hearing problem to carers who are not familiar with them, and if necessary outline the best ways of communicating with them. Make sure your relative has his or her spectacles and hearing aid; in a hospital or residential home it is wise to check unobtrusively from time to time that the earpiece is in the correct ear.

Whatever the person's mental state, good sight and hearing will help them to function as well as possible. Make sure your relative has an eye test at least every two years, and a hearing test if they seem to have trouble keeping track of conversations.

Although there are some drugs that produce a short-lived delay in the mental deterioration of Alzheimer's disease in its early stages, there is as yet no curative treatment. The brain damage that causes vascular dementia cannot be put right, but a small dose of aspirin may help to slow the rate of decline. However, in either condition the quality of life of both the person affected and their carer can be improved by good care. It will pay you to read up on the subject, so that you can ask for help in an informed way.

Dying at home

Many people say that when their time comes they would prefer to die in their own bed. Home has our personalities printed on it; it suits our own ideas of comfort and we can arrange our lives as we want them to be, rather than have to fit in with a hospital timetable. However, whether it is possible to stay at home during a last illness will depend on several factors: how much care the dying person needs, the abilities and fitness of the chief carer at home and how much help is available locally through health and social services. As the potential carer, there are several things you need to know to plan ahead sensibly. These include:

- What is wrong with the dying person?
- How long is this final illness likely to last? (It is impossible to be precise with this, but doctors should be able to give some rough guidance, such as days or weeks.)
- How will the progression of the illness affect the person's need for care, right up to the time of death?
- What services are available and how can you reach them?

Help at home

The GP will of course provide medical care, and there may be an outreach team from the local hospice to give technical advice on ways of coping with symptoms. The district nurse can provide nursing care, and is invaluable in teaching carers how to lift safely, to do dressings or to give injections. In some areas they also provide a 'twilight' or 'tucking in' service, visiting people in the evening and helping them to get ready for bed.

You may also be able to call on the services of a number of specialist nurses. This usually involves a referral from the GP or through the district nurse. Both Macmillan and Marie Curie nurses work with cancer patients and their families. Macmillan nurses advise on symptom control and provide counselling and support, whilst Marie Curie nurses provide more hands-on nursing care. Where appropriate, other specialist nurses such as the continence adviser and the stoma nurse may be called in. There may also be a care attendant from an organisation such as Crossroads, who can sit with a sick person and can help with their personal care but is not qualified to perform skilled nursing tasks. Alternatively, you could contact the UK Home Care Association (see p 144).

Help from social services

To obtain help from the social services department, the sick person or their carer or potential carer should ring the local office and ask to be referred to the person who does assessments; be warned that it may be some time before the assessment takes place. Possible services include help with personal care from a home carer, meals-on-wheels or another meals service, volunteer drivers for journeys to hospital appointments and possibly a laundry service to help with incontinence. The occupational therapist, also reached through social services, can advise about helpful aids and equipment (see the section on equipment, on pp 99–100), though again this can take some time. If the case manager or social worker who does the assessment has arranged for less services than you feel you need, you should appeal as described under 'Approaching social services' (p 87).

Benefits

There is a section on state benefits on pages 87–89. However, the rules for claiming Attendance Allowance are different for people who are terminally ill. The GP fills in a form that states that the person is so ill that they are not expected to live for more than six months. This is then processed quickly so that the benefit can be paid almost at once, rather than waiting for the usual six months since the need for care began.

Caring for someone in their final illness can be expensive. There may be a need for a substantial one-off payment for a piece of equipment such as a washing machine or tumble-dryer. Single payments of this sort can be made from the Benefit Agency's Social Fund as grants or loans. In addition, there are a number of charities that may help; for instance, Macmillan Cancer Relief and Marie Curie Cancer Care provide such help for people with cancer, while Counsel and Care concentrates on older people. There are also a number of service charities, such as the Royal British Legion and SSAFA (Soldiers, Sailors and Air Force Association), that will help the many older people who served in the forces. Your local public library will have a directory of charities, or the National Association of Councils for Voluntary Service (see p 139) may be able to help.

When care at home becomes impossible

Although it may be possible to start with care at home, later when the dying person's needs become more difficult to meet, a move to other accommodation may be necessary. The options are:

■ A nursing home, whose staff includes qualified nurses and can therefore provide a broad range of care.

■ A hospital; admission to hospital may be necessary if it becomes difficult to give all the appropriate care at home. There may be a 'palliative care' team to help the ward staff to look after the dying person and make sure they are as comfortable as possible.

■ A hospice; while hospices still provide care in the last stages of illness, they now offer other forms of care. These can include short admissions or attendance by the day to control symptoms, periods of respite care, an outreach or home care team and day care with activities and lunch. It is therefore often possible for the sick person to get to know the hospice and its staff while less severely ill, so that if a period of in-patient care becomes necessary both the staff and the surroundings are familiar.

Towards the end

There is of course no 'right' way of dying. Pain and discomfort can usually be made manageable, perhaps with advice from an NHS palliative care team, a hospice outreach team or a Macmillan nurse. As the end approaches, the sick person may have a number of needs, and the best thing is probably to give every possible opportunity for these to be made known. Some people need to say goodbye or to make their peace with family members and friends; others are concerned about the welfare of the family they leave behind – whether they have enough money, and whether they can cope with the tasks formerly done by the sick person. Some need their fears to be allayed – about severe pain or suffocating to death, or being left alone at the last; the doctor or nurse is often the best person to provide convincing reassurance here. Some people want spiritual help, even though they have shown no interest in religion for years. It may be easier for them to ask to see the appropriate religious leader if you have raised the subject in general terms already.

Because many people go into hospital when severely ill, it is now quite common for adults to have no experience of death. It is important for carers to know that an expected death is rarely gruesome; the dying person usually slips gently into unconsciousness. (The sense of hearing is the last to be lost, so it is important to be careful what is said near the deathbed.) The dying person's breathing becomes slower and shallower until it gradually stops. After this the person's body gradually becomes pale and cold.

After the death, if carers feel able to, they should remove surplus bedding, leaving only a single pillow and a covering sheet. The eyes should be gently closed, the arms straightened by the sides and the mouth held closed by a pillow or book under the chin. The doctor should be notified, and, after the death certificate has been filled in, the relative who will organise the funeral should get in touch with the undertaker, who will remove the body.

For further information, refer to Age Concern's book *Caring for someone who is dying* by Penny Mares, and Factsheet 27 *Arranging a funeral*.

Equipment to maintain independence or to help with home nursing

A great variety of aids are now available, and they can be very useful to a sick or disabled older person and to their carer. Unfortunately, the way equipment is supplied is often most unsatisfactory: similar equipment comes from different agencies, the system varies from place to place, and supply may take so long that the person's needs have changed by the time the now inappropriate aid arrives. In a few areas, a central equipment store has been set up. This supplies articles for people referred by both health and social services, and the system seems to have many advantages. Below is a guide to common patterns of supply under the traditional system.

Aids to help with daily living tasks

These include bath seats or boards or raised lavatory seats to help with personal hygiene; gadgets for cooking or eating, such as one-handed kitchen equipment or cutlery with built-up handles for arthritis sufferers; and products to make sitting or lying more comfortable. All these are usually supplied through the social services department, after an assessment by the occupational therapist. Some local authorities make a charge for such aids, while others supply them free. In some areas, smaller items are not supplied, so patients have to obtain for themselves any article costing, say, less than £20. On the other hand, larger items may be classed as adaptations and supplied by the housing department.

Mobility aids

Mobility aids include wheelchairs, walking sticks, zimmer frames and their variations. For a wheelchair, the patient is referred by the GP to the NHS Wheelchair Service. The chair is lent free, but there may be a deposit to pay. However, the choice is rather limited; there is, for instance, no electrically powered wheelchair for outdoor use available free on the NHS. The Wheelchair Service has a voucher system that will either meet the total cost of a basic wheelchair or can be put towards the price of a more expensive model.

It is helpful to have the advice of the physiotherapist or occupational therapist as to which wheelchair will be most useful, and the same is true for walking aids. However, there can be some delay, and sometimes the disabled person does not wish to wait for an assessment. If you are thinking of getting aids for yourself, do get the opinion of an expert (eg the district nurse or the physiotherapist) before making a purchase. It may be possible to see aids at a Disabled Living Centre near you.

Aids to home nursing

Special mattresses and sheepskins to prevent pressure sores may be available from the health authority, and the district nurse or GP will know how to obtain them. Other equipment includes urine bottles, bedpans, commodes, hoists and similar articles. It may also be possible to borrow a wheelchair for short-term or emergency use. These may be available through the district nurse on referral from the GP, or on loan from the local branch of the Red Cross. A hoist may sometimes be borrowed from the health authority's Home Loans Equipment Service, but those for long-term use are usually supplied through the social services department. Organisations such as the Round Table and other charities may be able to help. If you are thinking of buying a hoist privately, it is wise to get the opinion of an expert such as a physiotherapist or occupational therapist, and to make sure it is demonstrated in the home where it is to be used.

Feelings

These come unbidden into the carer's consciousness, and can often be surprisingly strong. Some feelings – tenderness, laughter, achievement – are pleasant, especially if they can be shared with the person cared for, and many people experience these, at least some of the time. On the whole, however, it is the negative feelings such as anger and misery that cause most difficulties, and these are the ones discussed below. Here are a few general principles for coping with negative feelings:

First, admit you have them. It is only human to feel irritated by someone who is behaving in an irritating way, even though you know that their behaviour is part of their illness. It is only human to become exasperated by inadequate service provision, or by the delays in paying benefits. Do not expect more from yourself than you would expect from a friend in a similar situation.

Second, find someone you can talk to, for the relief of 'getting it off your chest' and for the helpful experience of reviewing alternative options for the future. A family member may not be the best person, as they may be emotionally involved in the situation themselves. You really need someone you do not want to impress with your self-sacrifice or competence – someone to whom you can tell the plain, unvarnished truth. You may have a friend who fits the bill but, if not, you might like to attend your local carers' group, to try to find someone suitable.

Another possibility would be to find a professional counsellor. Counselling is not just fashionable nonsense, but neither is it the panacea for all ills. What it does offer is the chance to talk to someone who is outside your immediate circle and has no personal axe to grind, who will not be shocked or even surprised by what you have to say, who will respect your confidence and will help you to make your own decisions without interference. There may be a counsellor attached to your GP's practice, and your GP can refer you if they think you need it. Alternatively, you could ask at the Citizens Advice Bureau about counselling help from local charities or voluntary organisations. You can also arrange to see someone privately, but it is important to find out about their qualifications and the costs beforehand, as fees can be high. The British Association for Counselling and Psychotherapy (see p 133) can advise about counselling services in your area.

Third, consider the problems you have with caring and try to find out what could be done to lighten your load. There are a number of suggestions in this section, but you may also want to ask yourself, 'What is the worst thing?' and start from there.

If possible, aim to do a little less than you feel you can manage, and arrange for a little more help and respite than you feel you need. You might also want to read one of the books about caring mentioned in the booklist (see p 129).

Anger

Most carers feel angry from time to time. There may seem to be a great vat of seething anger inside, just waiting for something to raise the temperature a bit for the whole lot to boil over. Sometimes the overflow is unwittingly triggered by the person they are caring for, who may for instance have an episode of incontinence at a particularly inconvenient time; at other times it may be the inability of agencies such as social services departments to provide desperately needed help.

Other people's attitudes can be annoying; those who regard the carer as 'a saint' with inexhaustible patience, who can then tell themselves comfortably that there is no need for anyone else to get involved. An angry carer does not fit into this comfortable stereotype, so people do not want to know about the situation. The carer's own attitudes may be unhelpful: many people, especially women, had impressed on them as children that anger was a 'wrong' feeling, and should never be expressed. However, burying anger merely allows it to grow, and the eventual overflow will be larger. What is needed is to find a safe way of discharging anger. Below are some ways that others have found useful:

- Walk away from whoever or whatever caused your anger.
- Release your feelings safely – shout, jump up and down, punch a pillow, whatever helps.
- Try a relaxation technique; there is a simple one on page 28.
- If possible, switch off from your caring responsibilities for a while and do something that will distract your mind.
- If you often feel angry like this, you may want to think about action in the long term; see the section 'Breaking point' on page 89.

Tiredness

There are many reasons why you may feel tired. The practical duties of caring may use a good deal of physical energy, and mental energy can be depleted by the amount of organisation needed to fit in with services and keep a home running. Your relative's needs may lead to unpredictable interruptions that disrupt privacy and family life; in the worst case, this may happen at night, so your rest is broken, or you sleep lightly 'with one ear open', listening for a call.

When locked into an exhausting daily round, it is sometimes difficult to believe that anything can help. In considering the following suggestions, do not dismiss potentially helpful strategies without a little serious thought.

- Lower your standards a little, and do only essential domestic chores. Cut back on tasks such as ironing, and use convenience foods when this would help.
- Consider getting someone else to do some of the remaining work.
- If you feel you cannot afford the money needed for the suggestions above, check that you are receiving your full state benefit entitlements. Think also whether a piece of equipment such as a washing machine might make life easier; various charities give grants of lump sums for this sort of purpose. You will find a directory of grant-giving agencies at the public library.
- Try to fit in your sleeping pattern with that of your relative; if he or she is wakeful at night but takes a long nap after lunch, do the same.
- If you have trouble getting off to sleep, try the suggestions for inducing sleep on pages 29–30. Exercise in the day not only contributes to restful nights but also helps to reduce stress. Look also at the tips for stress management on pages 26–29.
- Ask for help from family and friends, stating exactly what you need; even well-disposed people may be reluctant to seem to interfere if they are not asked.
- Try to arrange some day care for your relative; then use the time to relax, rather than to catch up on the household chores.

Depression

We all get 'a bit down' from time to time: a little more rest, some time away from caring may be enough to put things right. More severe depression may be a sign that that the time for care at home has gone, and other forms of care must be considered. In its worst form, depression becomes an illness that impairs thought processes such as memory, concentration and decision-making, as well as plaguing the person affected with guilt, low self-esteem, inability to sleep from the small hours onwards and a low mood that can approach despair. People in this situation may be told by those around them to 'pull themselves together' and 'look on the bright side', which is about as helpful as telling someone with a broken leg to run round the block. Depression of this sort needs urgent medical treatment; however, people with depression may not realise this themselves and may need prompting and help from family and friends to seek the help they need.

You can find out more about depression on pages 56–57.

Guilt

All human relationships are flawed; when we think of the people we love best we can all remember things that we wish had not been said and done. In the close quarters of caring these feelings are intensified, and in addition there are other sources of guilt. Some people have caring thrust on them and feel they were trapped into it; they hate their daily round, and then start to hate themselves for feeling that way. Other carers worry that they are not caring as well as they should, and feel guilty because of it. Some people are the filling in the 'care sandwich', with young people one side and older ones the other. Trying to spread themselves impossibly thin, carers like these describe their lives as endlessly deciding whom to let down next. Perhaps the worst guilt of all is felt by carers who become unable to carry on and have to help their relative move into residential care. Conscientious people too often view this as 'I let Mother down' rather than 'I looked after Mother for as long as I possibly could'.

It may help to remember that these feelings are not necessarily a sign of wrongdoing. Thinking of the situation and wondering how you would advise a friend in a similar situation may reveal the guilt as inappropriate. It will not necessarily evaporate at once, but it may become possible to counter every guilty feeling with reality by thinking 'I do not deserve to feel guilty because I am doing my best'. Gradually the guilt feelings should become weaker. Many people will want to talk about their feelings, and the suggestions about finding someone to talk to at the beginning of this section should help them to find someone suitable (see p 101).

Religious doubts

Carers who attend a place of worship regularly may find that some fellow worshippers choose to believe that carers are so dedicated and so self-sacrificing that they rise above all difficulties. No support is then forthcoming except lip service, and certainly no one offers an accepting, non-judgemental ear for confidences about anger, tiredness and other negative feelings. However, there will be others in the worshipping community who are well-intentioned, and who may even have caring experience themselves. These may well take some of the load off a carer, but may not offer in case they are thought to 'interfere'. It will probably be best for carers to ask a religious leader whether the community includes any likely volunteers, and also whether there are any official activities available – a day centre, for instance.

Carers may also horrify themselves by feeling angry with God for letting their painful situation come about. This is best discussed with the appropriate religious leader. One response in such a situation was 'Don't worry. God can take it!' – a remark that is not as flippant and facetious as it sounds at first.

Loneliness

As many carers know, it is possible to feel lonely when never actually alone. Many relatives have personalities that have changed through illnesses such as Alzheimer's disease or stroke, so they are no longer good company. Others may have had quite different lifestyles and interests from the people who now care for them: it is quite possible, for instance, to love your husband or father dearly but not to share his passion for cricket, or to find his choice of music irritating beyond bearing. There are many reasons why the person you care for cannot provide enough human contact in themselves.

It takes effort to keep old friendships in good repair, but the results are worth it. Most of us have old friends for whom it is no longer necessary to put up a front. We can tell them our real feelings, and we feel comfortable about asking them to call on us in our less than perfect homes. This is usually easier to arrange than to organise sitters while you go out; however, when your relative shows really difficult or bizarre behaviour, taking some time off away from home may be the best option.

Some carers complain that no one ever visits them, while unwittingly behaving in a way that deters casual callers. People may stay away because they do not want to disturb a rest or a bath, or because they feel embarrassed about not calling before, or because they do not want to make extra work. The answer here is a clear invitation, for instance to 'come for coffee at 11 o'clock, before I give Clive his dinner at 1pm'. When visitors do arrive, they should not be greeted with a tight-lipped 'Hello, stranger!' however long since their last call; 'How nice to see you!' is far more likely to make the visitor want to come again. Try to have some topics of conversation apart from the ups and downs of caring; it is usually possible to find an opportunity to glance at the newspaper headlines or to watch the television news.

It is also wise to join a local carers' support group (see p 124). Apart from finding the meetings helpful in themselves, you may be able to make new friends among people who understand the difficulties of caring and the problems you are going through.

Other strategies include spotting good and bad times and trying to identify helpful and unhelpful factors. Then pursue the one and avoid the other. Finally, do persevere: loneliness is unpleasant in itself, but also it makes anxiety, tiredness and stress harder to bear.

General health of your relative

- Try to make sure that your relative takes advantage of the over-75 health check, which should be offered by the GP once a year. As well as medical problems, this check might identify 'social' needs that could be met by the stimulation of a day centre or reveal that your relative is eligible for an unclaimed benefit.
- While of course allowing your relative to see the doctor or other health worker alone if they so wish, try to have a brief interview with the doctor yourself. This will enable you to pass on useful information that your relative might have forgotten and to ask general questions about

her or his care, though the doctor will need to keep some medical details confidential.

■ It is wise to make sure your relative's medicines are reviewed by the doctor at least once a year and preferably every six months, with unnecessary pills and potions being stopped. It may help the doctor if you and your relative together collect up all the medicines into a plastic bag (or on a tray for a home visit), so that the size and nature of the problem is apparent.

■ Someone with a dementing illness may function less well than usual if they develop a physical illness such as a chest or urinary infection, or if they are suffering unwanted effects from their medicines. If you think this might be happening, ask your doctor to give your relative a physical check.

■ A sight test at least every two years, and more often if problems arise, will help your relative to identify what is going on around him or her, and will make it easier to avoid hazards that might lead to an accident such as a fall.

■ Poor hearing can also worsen confusion as well as spoiling social life. Encourage your relative to seek help, as problems such as accumulated wax in the ear can easily be solved. If a hearing aid is necessary, give support in getting used to it, and check whether there is a local domiciliary service for replacing batteries and doing minor repairs.

■ A sore mouth and ill-fitting dentures can restrict an older person to eating only soft food, and thus lead to poor nutrition. It can also make it difficult for them to speak and be understood. Even someone with no teeth of their own should have a check at least once a year to make sure their mouth is healthy and their dentures still fit.

■ Sore feet with tender corns, hard skin and neglected toenails are painful to walk on, so their owner may wear loose cloth slippers and avoid going out. A visit to the chiropodist can result in a great improvement in mobility, as well as making the older person steadier on his or her feet.

Giving up caring

Eventually the need to be a carer passes: the person cared for moves into other accommodation such as a residential home or dies. Even if such an event is expected, it can evoke powerful feelings. When your relative has moved, your main feeling may be guilt at having 'failed' him or her at the last, forgetting the months or years of loving caring that went before it. If you are in this situation, remember instead that you did your best for as long as you could, which is all anyone can do. You may be helped by a carers' group or by a counsellor, often available through your GP or CRUSE or through the National Association of Bereavement Services.

When the person you cared for has died, you may suffer from the same sorts of distress as any other person who has suffered a loss (see 'Loss and bereavement', p 30). In addition there may be other complicating factors, such as a powerful feeling of relief, which may shock you. This is especially likely if the dead person's illness changed their personality or behaviour, or if they were weakened by pain or distress before they died. Now, suddenly, you can go out without making elaborate arrangements for a sitter, the stress and the responsibility are gone and there are no interruptions to a night's sleep – except a long-standing tendency to sleep lightly even though the need for it has gone. Feelings like these are best talked about with a close and understanding friend or with a counsellor or other professional, or at a carers' group.

Anger is common in these situations, as at the time of most losses, and it may be directed at God, or fate, or at the services that were felt not to be there to provide the right help at the right time. Sometimes a formal complaint may be appropriate, while at others the anger will subside as time passes; discussion with a trusted and knowledgeable person, such as the secretary of the community health council, can help in deciding what to do.

Once the acute distress has died down a little, many ex-carers feel lost and lonely. Caring may have given a structure to the day; the cared-for person, even if difficult, was someone to wake up for, someone to come home to, someone to talk to – even if they were not always able to understand or to reply coherently. Coping with this requires a little planning, which is often best done in advance and on paper. Try, for instance, to have a reason to go out every day; this gives a fresh perspective on the neighbourhood, as well as a reason to get properly dressed and groomed. Make the effort to rebuild a social circle, perhaps starting with those of your old friends you would like to see more of. If embarrassment or concerns not to intrude have been keeping them away, a simple invitation to 'Come round for tea on Thursday at about 4 o'clock so we can catch up on the news' may help. Making new friends is often easier as a by-product of another activity, and you may want to consider enrolling for a class, taking up voluntary work or joining a carers' group or another support agency for the condition that affected your relative.

Gradually things should improve as the distressing feelings fade, life regains its interest and times of spontaneous enjoyment become ever more frequent. If this does not happen, however, and you feel miserable and unable to move on from your past life, it is important you see your doctor so that you can be treated medically or, if necessary, referred for specialist help.

Home from hospital

All hospital patients dream of coming home to their own bed. However, if the correct arrangements are not made in good time, the dream can become a nightmare. To prevent this happening, it is best to start thinking about the return home as soon as your relative has gone into hospital in the first place.

Every hospital is required to have a discharge procedure to ensure that vulnerable people do not find themselves at home too early or with insufficient care. Among other things, the procedure should involve the GP and social services, and ensure that:

- the person's needs have been assessed;
- any equipment they need has been installed, and help and support have been arranged before they are discharged;
- both the person and their carer are fully informed about these arrangements and of when the person is to leave hospital;
- the GP and district nurse have been given enough information about the person's hospital care so that they are able to take over at home without a disruptive gap.

If the social services department will be responsible for providing services (including some nursing care), a charge may be made to your relative.

Anything provided by the NHS, however (eg specialist nursing care), will be free. When the social services department is involved in the assessment, you can also request an assessment for yourself.

Problems mainly seem to come about when the procedure fails, but there are ways of reducing the likelihood of this happening. While your relative is in hospital, try to get to know the ward staff. The head nurse may be male or female, and may be called the ward sister, the charge nurse or the ward manager. In some hospitals your relative will be looked after by a named nurse, responsible for co-ordinating his or her nursing care. Both of these are good people to ask how discharge planning is going, and to tell of your misgivings, if any, about your relative's ability to manage at home again. It will be useful to arrange your visits to coincide with times when these staff are on duty.

The assessment process to identify your relative's needs may be conducted partly at home, usually by a physiotherapist or occupational therapist. The assessment aims to find out how your relative manages in real circumstances, and it may be a useful time for you to be present. Sometimes you will be surprised and pleased by your relative's new-found skills, while at others you may be able to set the record straight if your relative, in their enthusiasm to come home, exaggerates the amount of support the family is able to provide.

You may also be invited to a case conference, in which hospital staff and those from the community come together to make sure that the person's care is not disrupted by the discharge process. If this has been arranged and you have not been invited, you should ask to attend. Before the case conference takes place, you should be shown the results of the assessment. After the conference you should receive written details of what has been agreed, including the name of a 'nominated individual' whom you can contact for further explanation or if you are unhappy about the assessment.

If you think your relative is being discharged prematurely or with inadequate help and support, you should say so to the ward sister and/or the named nurse. If necessary, you should also ask to see the consultant, the senior doctor in charge of your relative's care. It is your right as carer to ask for a review of the hospital's discharge arrangements. If it is suggested that you should have your relative home to live with you, remember that you can refuse to do so if you do not wish it or if you fear that the services arranged are insufficient; this may distress your relative, so will obviously be a last resort. If in spite of your efforts your relative is discharged prematurely, you should use the hospital's complaints procedure; the community health council or the Citizens Advice Bureau can help with this.

Home safety

Most of the accidents that befall older people occur at home, but the removal of hazards and the addition of safety equipment can reduce the chances of such mishaps. Checking for danger points is comparatively easy, as is putting things right if the home is yours. However, no one likes to be told how to run their own home, and, if that is where your relative is living, it will take great tact to bring about any alteration. Below are some possible causes of accidents to check on.

- Trip hazards, such as torn or uneven carpets or loose rugs, loose stair-rods, footstools and doorstops.
- Lack of handrails in bathroom or lavatory and on both sides of the staircase.
- Lack of non-slip mats in the bath or shower.
- Wearing inappropriate footwear around the house. Shoes with non-slip soles should be worn; slippers are best kept for the bedroom.
- Poor lighting in halls or on landings; substitute high wattage bulbs, and explain that the increase in cost is marginal.
- Trailing electrical flex, which should be secured, while checking that sockets are not over-loaded with adapters and plugs.
- A gas cooker or other appliance that your relative frequently fails to light; you may be able to substitute a self-lighting version or, if your relative is confused, to have a control fitted which only you can work. You may also want to consider a change to an electric or microwave oven, though your relative may find the new equipment difficult to understand.
- An absence of smoke detectors.
- Medicines left lying about, which are especially dangerous if your relative is confused.

An occupational therapist can advise about useful equipment. It may be possible to obtain equipment through the social services department or the health authority, or it can be obtained and fitted privately (see 'Equipment to maintain independence or to help with home nursing', p 99). Larger repairs or adaptations can sometimes be organised by a Foundation or Staying Put team, both of which help an older person claim appropriate grants to fund works and to supervise their completion. Your local Age Concern organisation will know whether there is one of these in your district, or you could try looking in the telephone directory.

Incontinence

Someone who has lost control of their bladder or bowels can be unpleasant to look after, and this is sometimes the point at which carers decide they cannot manage any longer. However, many cases of incontinence can be put right, and more can be made tolerable by the use of up-to-date equipment. Below are a few points to remember.

Urinary incontinence

Old age is not in itself a cause of incontinence, though the passing of the years does mean that less has to go wrong before control is lost. The GP should be asked to examine the incontinent person, looking for causes of the problem. Common ones include urinary infections, diabetes, constipation (which can cause bowel incontinence as well), gynaecological problems such as prolapse in women and prostate enlargement in men. Diagnosing and treating these conditions may improve the incontinence, or even get rid of it altogether. For more details, see pages 70–72.

The doctor may refer your relative to the continence adviser, who is a nurse with extra training in the causes and management of incontinence. You can also contact your continence adviser direct; you can find the telephone number through the health centre, district nurse or health visitor, or from the community health council. The continence adviser can suggest ways of coping with the situation from day to day, and can recommend suitable pads, pants and similar equipment if necessary. These may be available free from the health authority, but arrangements differ around the country. In addition, some local authorities run an incontinence laundry service or a special collection service for soiled pads. You can find out what is available in your area by ringing your local social services department.

Bowel incontinence

This is often the last straw on the carer's load. Nearly all cases are due to severe constipation, with soft or liquid faeces leaking past the accumulated mass of stool. A few cases come about because the person has diarrhoea and cannot reach the lavatory in time, and fewer still because the muscle ring, or sphincter, that closes the end of the bowel at the anus has been damaged or is ineffective, as in people with a rectal prolapse.

The cause of the bowel incontinence can usually be found if the person is examined by a doctor or nurse. In most cases the hard mass of stool will need to be removed by enemas or, occasionally, manually. To stop the condition recurring, the amount of fruit, vegetables and other high-fibre foods (see p 2) in the diet should be increased and more fluids drunk. It may also help to look at the medicines the person is taking – both those prescribed and those bought over the counter – as these commonly contribute to constipation. Common culprits are codeine in cough mixtures, many pain-killers and some antidepressants. Sometimes a regular dose of a laxative will also be necessary.

If the person has diarrhoea, the cause must be found and treated. The doctor will identify 'medical' ones, but there are some others. A common one is the excessive use of laxatives by an older person who was brought up on the belief that 'a good clearout' every day is essential to health. A very tactful and non-patronising approach is needed to suggest that a change in diet and more fluids might be more helpful. Diarrhoea can sometimes be a sign that a confused person who hates what she or he thinks of as 'waste' has been eating spoiled food. This is a sign that a tactful relative or 'home help' should clean out the fridge from time to time.

The small proportion of people with bowel incontinence who have sphincter problems at the anus will need to be seen by a surgeon, to be considered for operation.

More information about incontinence and ways of coping with it is available from the Continence Foundation (address on p 135).

Living wills

These are sometimes called advance directives. They are documents in which people who are of sound mind describe what they would like to happen to them if at some future date they become too ill to decide for themselves. An older woman might, for instance, write in her advance directive that, if she has a moderately severe dementia, she would not want to be resuscitated from a cardiac arrest or to receive antibiotics for pneumonia. The person making the living will cannot require a doctor to do anything that is not lawful – for instance, to end the person's life. In other words, a living will does not ask or allow a doctor to participate in 'mercy killing'.

Of course, people who are not mentally impaired must consent before treatment can be given. Similarly, they can refuse treatment that they do not want, even though they are then likely to die. An advance directive has the same legal force, provided that the statement applies to their current circumstances, and that there is no reason to suppose that they have changed their mind. These conditions are sometimes difficult to fulfil: people's views about their treatment often seem to change as their illness progresses, or they may become ill or disabled in a way they had not previously foreseen. There may then be real doubt as to whether the directive still applies. Although doctors are permitted to act in the 'best interests' of a patient who cannot consent, when there is doubt as to what these best interests are, they should consult experienced colleagues and, if necessary, seek legal advice. Rarely, they may be advised to go to court for a ruling.

It is always wise for people who have written advance directives to review them regularly, and make whatever changes they see fit. It is also important that relatives or friends and the GP know that these documents exist and where to find them.

Managing someone else's money

This section will be of interest if your relative is no longer able to collect their pension or other benefits, or if they are becoming or have become too mentally confused to cope with their own financial affairs.

Collecting the pension

Your relative, if they so wish, can nominate you as their 'agent' to collect their pension on their behalf. If this is a temporary measure, they can simply complete the declaration on the back of the pension order. If, on the other hand, the arrangement is likely to be permanent, they can apply for a card authorising their agent (you) to collect the pension on their behalf; further details can be obtained from the Benefits Agency. Please note that your relative must be fully aware of what they are doing when they ask you to act as their agent; an 'agency' arrangement cannot therefore be used when the person is too confused to manage their own affairs. However, in these circumstances the Benefits Agency can appoint someone to receive the confused person's benefits and to spend them on their behalf. This 'appointeeship' is used only in relation to state benefits; if the person has other income or has capital, an enduring power of attorney may be necessary or, if the person has 'lost mental capacity', the Court of Protection may need to become involved.

Power of attorney

This is a legal document completed by one person, the 'donor', which entitles another person, the 'attorney', to act on their behalf. It can give general powers to manage all of the donor's affairs, or can apply to a single operation, such as selling a house. This sort of power of attorney can operate only as long as the donor is mentally capable of managing their affairs; if they develop a dementia, for instance, it automatically becomes invalid.

Enduring power of attorney

This document entitles the attorney to act after the donor has become too confused to manage their own affairs. However, it must be organised and signed while the donor still understands what they are doing and how it will work. Unless the enduring power of attorney (EPA) is restricted, it can be used as soon as it has been signed by all parties and their signatures have been witnessed. If and when the donor becomes or is becoming confused, the attorney notifies the Public Trust Office to have the EPA registered. They must also tell the donor and at least three near relatives that this is being done. Once the document has been returned registered, the EPA gives authority to act, and can be shown to banks and similar organisations for this purpose. The Public Trustee oversees the operation of the EPA, and any complaints about its operation should be addressed to that officer.

Court of Protection

This office deals with the financial affairs of people who are too mentally impaired to undertake them themselves, and who have not taken out an enduring power of attorney. The Court of Protection operates by appointing a 'receiver' to deal with the confused person's everyday affairs; the receiver is usually a close relative or friend, but can also be a lawyer, a bank or a local authority. The arrangements the receiver makes on the donor's behalf are overseen by the Public Trustee, and large or important transactions need the Court's or the Trustee's consent. There are various types of Order, depending on the amount of capital involved and how simple or complicated the person's financial affairs are.

The receiver is concerned only with the donor's business affairs, and has no control over his or her person; the receiver cannot, for instance, give consent to a medical procedure on the donor's behalf.

The Public Trust Office produces a number of booklets explaining these rather complicated arrangements; they are available from the Public Trust Office's Customer Services Unit (Mental Health), Protection Division (see p 140).

Pressure sores

These happen in people who are lying in bed or sitting in a chair and who are unable to move about. The soft tissues become compressed between bony protuberances, such as the sacrum (base of the spine) and the bed or chair. Other vulnerable areas include the heel, the back of the head and the elbows. Blood is unable to flow through the squashed tissues, and if the pressure is not relieved the tissues may break down into a wound that is difficult to heal. While caring for the older person, you may notice that the skin over a bony point has become red and dry; this is a sign that a pressure sore is threatening to form, and the district nurse or GP should be notified without delay.

To prevent pressure sores, the person at risk must be advised to change their position every two hours; if they are unable to do this, they should be turned as often as practicable. It may also be helpful to borrow, hire or buy a pressure-relieving system such as a 'ripple' mattress; the Disabled Living Centre or the district nurse will know how to go about this, and will advise on the choice of equipment. It is of course helpful to keep the person's general health as good as possible; in particular, make sure they are not anaemic and that their diet contains adequate protein and vitamin C.

Respite breaks

All carers need time to themselves, when they can rest and restore their energies, knowing that the person they usually care for is safe and well looked after. Substitute carers may be available to take over for short periods, such as an afternoon, or for longer times, for instance to cover a fortnight's holiday. Help with caring of this sort is in short supply, so it is wise to start making arrangements in good time, especially in the holiday season. What is on offer varies from place to place, so a certain amount of research is necessary to discover what is available to you in your area. It is also sensible to work out what sort of break you need, and of course to discuss the matter with your relative as far as possible. Some of the commonest forms of respite are outlined below.

Sitting services

Crossroads is probably the best known of these schemes. The service exists primarily to provide support for carers, and staff try to care for the older person in the same way that the usual carer does. They may sit with the person concerned for a few hours, or cover a longer period such as the carer's admission to hospital. You should find your local branch of the Crossroads Association in the telephone book, or you could get in touch with the head office (see p 135). In addition, there may be other similar groups working in your area, and your local social services department should have details of them all; social services may, in fact, be able to offer a sitting service.

Paying your own helper

This can be expensive. You can organise help through an agency or employ someone yourself. The agency costs more, but it has two advantages. First, the complex paperwork that goes with taking on an employee will be done for you. Secondly, if your usual helper is not available, the agency will provide someone else. If you decide to employ your own helper, you may like to ask your Citizens Advice Bureau for advice on fulfilling your duties as an employer.

A volunteer bureau

People with time to spare may be willing to sit with an older person. You could find out about such services from the Citizens Advice Bureau or the public library.

Relatives and friends

It is worth asking yourself whether you are getting all the help you could from the rest of your relative's family and circle. Sometimes they do not want to be involved, but in other cases you may seem to be doing everything so well that they do not know what help to offer, or fear that they will be rebuffed if they try to do so. Do not be too proud to ask for help, and specify exactly what you need. If you are hoping that another family member could take over your caring role for a while, you should think a little about practical details. For instance, if your relative needs the stair lift to go up to bed and a variety of rails and other equipment in the bathroom to use it independently, it would make more sense for another family member to move into your house in your absence than for your relative to move into their unadapted home.

Day centres

These offer a number of activities, sometimes with bathing, hairdressing and chiropody. People attending are given a midday meal and hot drinks morning and afternoon, and transport to and from the centre is often provided. Unfortunately, the hours of the day centre are not usually long enough to free the carer for a full day's work. You can find out about day centres from the social services department, and your relative can apply for a place by asking to be assessed for one.

Holidays

Holidays can be arranged so that your relative goes away alone, or that you go away together but staff take over some caring duties; this means you have some time to yourself. RADAR and Holiday Care (see pp 141 and 137) can provide information as to what is available and how to find the money to pay for it. In addition, some social services departments organise holidays or make grants towards their costs.

You go on holiday while your relative is cared for elsewhere There are a few schemes by which an older person stays with a specially trained family, who are paid to look after them while the usual carer has a weekend or a longer period away. This may be worth considering if either you or your relative is very reluctant to consider a brief stay in a residential or nursing home. Ask the social services department whether there is such a scheme in your area.

Someone who has complex health or nursing needs may be entitled to respite care in a nursing home, hospice or even a hospital, though this is much less common than it used to be. You could discuss this sort of care with one of your relative's doctors; for information about hospice care, ring the Hospice Information Service (p 137).

A respite break in a residential home is arranged through the social services department. The staff will assess your relative's needs and yours, and, if a place is offered, they may be able to help financially.

Carers are sometimes reluctant to suggest that their relative has a respite stay in a residential or nursing home. However, as with other forms of respite, a break of this sort can enable the carer to carry on at home for longer. If the relative needs to move to the home at a later date, the familiarity that comes from earlier respite breaks helps to make the move easier. Moreover, the relative might welcome a break, too.

Risk taking

There is no such thing as a risk-free life. In a normal day, most of us walk up and down stairs, use electrical equipment, drive a car or go by public transport, cross roads and so on; all these activities carry small risks but they are the price we are prepared to pay for a full and rewarding life. When caring for an older person, we often feel very protective, and this can make it difficult to tolerate the sort of behaviour we would find quite normal in someone 30 years younger. Although these feelings are good in themselves, they can sometimes be harmful. They may lead to restrictions being placed on an older person's freedom and independence, ostensibly 'to keep them safe', but in truth, to safeguard our peace of mind.

Of course, an older person who is mentally 'intact' (mentally capable) has the same right to make his or her own decisions and to take the consequences as any other adult. When your relative does this, emphasising that you respect their decisions even when you do not agree with them will often make it easier for them to give way a little. As well as rights, they also have the same obligation to consider the feelings of others as anyone else, preferably in a practical way. For instance, it may help a concerned family a great deal if the older person agrees to make or receive a telephone call at a pre-arranged time each week to confirm that all is well.

It is far more difficult to give someone a reasonable amount of freedom when they have a mild to moderate dementing illness. The duty to allow them as much self-determination as possible is directly opposed by the duty to protect them – an uncomfortable state of affairs. It is worth remembering that the 'capacity' to act responsibly and the ability to make choices are not all-or-nothing matters; someone who could not possibly manage their own investments can still choose whether to have sugar in their tea.

By thinking clearly, it may be feasible to make sure your relative enjoys as much independence and as many choices as possible in their life, without them or their carers feeling too anxious or worried about it. One way of thinking things out is outlined below.

Suppose your relative is doing something that makes you fear for their safety; work out the answers to the following questions:

- What are the risks to your relative?
- What are the risks, if any, to their property?
- What are the risks, if any, to others?
- What are the risks or disadvantages in terms of quality of life of your relative *not* behaving in the worrying way?
- Looking at the behaviour, are there any ways of modifying it?
- ... or of reducing its risks?
- Considering all the above factors, and taking into account the views of other carers and family members, what seems the best course of action?
- What does your relative think?
- Is it possible to work out a compromise?

Here are some examples of possible compromises.

> Mrs A is a very alert lady of 80 who enjoys shopping. She likes to pay in cash, and carries large sums of money in her handbag. Her family are worried that she will be mugged, and want her to stay at home while they do her shopping for her.

Risks to Mrs A? A risk of harm if robbed.

Risks to Mrs A's property? The money is unsafe, whether at home or in her handbag.

Risks to others? None.

Risks of staying indoors and not going shopping? Enormous, including loss of mobility and, more importantly, loss of interest in life.

The shopping itself does not give rise to anxiety – it is the lack of care with money, and this could be modified.

On balance, the best course of action would seem to be to stop nagging about the shopping and concentrate on safeguarding the money in a bank. Mrs A's views on this could be sought, and a relative could start a discussion on interest rates and the convenience of credit cards.

Mrs B is 75 and her sight has deteriorated considerably because of glaucoma. She lives in a rural area, and her car has been a great help to her in getting about. The family have only just realised that she is still driving, and wonder what to do.

Risks to Mrs B? An increased risk of an accident because of her poor sight.

Risks to Mrs B's property? The car has an increased risk of crash damage.

Risks to other people? Considerable, particularly to pedestrians.

Risks of not driving? Unfortunately, less activity and self-determination for Mrs B.

Unfortunately, there seems to be no way of modifying the behaviour to reduce its risks. There is no doubt here that Mrs B really should not drive – the risk to other people is too great, as well as that to herself.

The family and her GP should get together to help her make the decision herself with as little loss of face as possible. Only if she continues to drive against medical advice will the GP have to consider notifying the Driver and Vehicle Licensing Authority in Swansea.

To help her stay active even when not driving, more information about public transport and taxis is needed. When they are worked out, the costs of taxis may be less than the running costs of the car, and this may make a good face-saving excuse for giving up the car.

Miss C is a frail lady of 85 who has moderately severe dementia. She lives in a residential home where she is able to walk about independently, but has had several falls. Her only relative is her widowed niece, Mrs M, who has discovered that the staff have been told to wheel Miss C to meals and the lavatory in a wheelchair and discourage her from other activity in case she falls. If Miss C protests, they say, she can always be given 'something to quieten her'. Mrs M wonders what ought to be done.

Risks to Miss C of being independent? Injury from falls, including broken bones.

Risks to Miss C's property? None.

Risks to others? Danger of criticism or disciplinary action if Mss C breaks a bone or is otherwise injured.

Risks of not moving about? Considerable, including incontinence when not going to the lavatory as required without assistance, pressure sores, an increased risk of chest infection and a loss of interest in life. All these would become even more likely if she were to be sedated.

To reduce the risks of Miss C's activity it would be sensible to try to stop her from falling. If she saw her doctor, it might be possible to increase her stability if her medicines were reviewed and other 'medical' causes sought. Mrs M might consider other factors that she may be able to do something about, such as trip hazards, including worn slippers, loose mats, draught excluders and footstools (see p 111).

Even if the falls continue, there seems little doubt that Miss C will have a better quality of life if she is allowed and encouraged to keep active and mobile. Mrs M should discuss this with the head of the home, and emphasise that immobility can be more dangerous than the possibility of falls.

> Mr D, aged 80, has moderate vascular dementia. He lives with his daughter and son-in-law, and worries them by wandering off and sometimes having difficulty in finding his way back. Otherwise he seems to enjoy life, and spends hours pottering in the garden. The son-in-law thinks Mr D should move into a home, where he will be safer.

Risks to Mr D? Being mugged as a 'soft' target; falling and not being able to get up, perhaps developing hypothermia; and being run over.

Risks to Mr D's property? None.

Risks to other people? Might he cause an accident?

Risks of being moved to a place where there will be more restrictions? Great loss of quality of life; probably an increase in the risk of wandering in a strange area.

Note There is no evidence that people with dementia are more likely to be involved in road accidents than other older people, and they rarely come to other physical harm.

Mr D might be less likely to wander if someone were found to take him for walks. It might also help to note the circumstances that lead to him wandering, and either avoid them or be ready to distract him. Risks from wandering could be reduced by giving Mr D an identity bracelet or necklet carrying his name and a contact telephone number. If he usually goes to the same place, the people who are there now will often, if notified of Mr D's state, be prepared to telephone the family when he arrives. It may also help to have a recent photograph of him when looking for him.

Support groups

These offer two things: emotional support and practical help. Many carers find carers' groups invaluable psychologically and emotionally. Other group members have had experiences similar to their own, they know about the difficulties and small exasperations of caring and they do not pass judgement on other carers. Although new members will initially receive help, as time passes and their job as carer draws to a close, they can start to offer support to others in turn.

Apart from putting the carer in touch with others in a similar position, many groups give practical help. This may include:

- Providing information about the condition affecting the person who is cared for, or about specific difficulties, such as incontinence.
- Sharing information about local services, and representing the interests of carers and service users when services are planned.
- Sometimes providing sitters and care attendants; some will do this only while carers' groups are meeting and some will do it at other times as well.
- Supporting carers by home visits when they are not able to get away, advising about professional services such as counselling, and in due course providing companionship when the relative dies.

Some support groups are local branches of national associations, such as the Carers National Association, the Stroke Association or the Alzheimer's Society. The section 'Useful addresses' later in this book lists a number of such organisations. People at the national address will be able to direct you to your nearest branch, or you could look in the local telephone book. In some areas carers' groups are run by community health staff or by the social services department. To find these local groups, ask at the GP practice or the community health services trust, the Citizens Advice Bureau, the social services department or the public library.

Instead of joining an established group, you might simply want to meet one or a few other carers. You could ask the GP or district nurse if they know of anyone suitable, or ask if you may put a notice up in places where carers might see them, such as your GP's practice or health centre or at a day centre. For further advice on setting up your own group, get in touch with the Carers National Association (see p 135).

Wills

There are two good reasons for making a Will. One is that it ensures that the money and possessions of the person concerned are distributed in the way he or she would have wanted. The other is that it shortens and simplifies the job of winding up the dead person's affairs for the people left behind. This can be a time-consuming business when the person has died intestate (without having made a Will). Try to suggest that your relative make a Will if they have not already done so. If you have not made one either, this would be a good chance for you both to get it done.

Although forms for making your own Will are available, it is usually wise to consult a solicitor; the Citizens Advice Bureau should be able to suggest a suitable one who practices locally. Free legal advice may be available to some older people with disabilities who have little money, under the Legal Advice and Assistance Green Form Scheme. More details are available from the Citizens Advice Bureau.

Further information can be obtained from Age Concern's Factsheets 7 *Making your Will* and 14 *Dealing with someone's estate*.

Endpiece

Good health is not, of course, an end in itself. However, poor health – mobility problems, a tendency to fall, incontinence and, worst of all, confusion – can interfere with all the duties and pleasures of life. Good health, like running water, is only valued when it is no longer there.

It is sometimes said that the most important life choice we could make would be to choose our parents. The genes we inherit from our parents affect our health, but we can do nothing to alter our inheritance. This is true as far as it goes, but the lifestyle we adopt – the food we eat, whether we take exercise, how much alcohol we drink and whether we smoke – has as great an effect on our future.

Retirement can be a time when life changes may lead to real distress, often to the great surprise of the retired person, who had thought that life would feel like holiday all the time. The secret seems to be careful preparation, together with a willingness to make peace with the past – not always comfortable at the time but rewarding later.

If we become ill, most of us would like to be partners in our own care. For this to happen, we must know enough about the function of our bodies to be able to discuss treatment options with doctors and other health professionals in a sensible way. Good doctors usually like to work with well-informed patients; it is sad that time pressures sometimes provide very little discussion time.

Caring is always stressful and sometimes distressing, and health and social services provision to lighten the load is never generous. It does help, however, to know what might be on offer and how to mobilise possible sources of help. What is more, the support of other carers who have faced the same difficulties is often, so carers say, the most useful help of all.

If you are an older person, do not feel pressured into putting up with second-class treatment. People who are now retired have lived through difficult times, and have worked hard to set up the services from which the whole community now benefits. Good health care and adequate social services are not luxuries for older people; they are simply what they have earned and well deserve.

Glossary

Terms given in *italic* in the definition are also defined in this Glossary

acute in the context of illness, something that lasts only a short time (see also *chronic*)

aneurysm bulging weak point in a blood vessel

atheroma fatty deposit in the blood vessels, causing them to 'fur up'

biopsy taking a small sample of tissue to examine it to see if disease is present

chronic in the context of illness, something that lasts a long time (see also *acute*)

field of vision the area you can see when looking straight ahead (see also *peripheral vision*)

palpitations an uncomfortable awareness of the heartbeat

peripheral vision what you can see around the edges of your *field of vision*

placebo a 'medicine' that has no active ingredients but is given to someone to see if they get better because they believe it has

primary growth the original cancerous growth (see also *secondary growth*)

secondary growth cancerous growth that has developed because the original *primary growth* has spread

Further reading

Books published by commercial publishers can be borrowed from a library or bought in bookshops. For books published by national organisations, please refer to the section on 'Useful addresses' on pp 131–144 for their contact details. For free leaflets, send a large stamped, addressed envelope or label.

Eating well

The BBC Diet (1988) by Dr Barry Lynch, published by BBC Books, London

Healthy Eating on a Budget (1995) by Sara Lewis and Dr Juliet Gray, published by Age Concern Books, London

Sensible drinking

Alcohol and Older People: Safe drinking for the over 60s; from Alcohol Concern, free.

Smoking

Give Up pack; from ASH, free.

Exercise

Fitness for Life (1996) by Susie Dinan and Dr Craig Sharp, published by Judy Piatkus, London

Sex and relationships

Living, Loving and Ageing: Sexual and personal relationships in later life (1989) by Wendy Greengross and Sally Greengross, published by Age Concern Books, London. [Now out of print but may be available at your local library.]

Mind and spirit

Help is at Hand leaflets; a range of titles including Bereavement, Depression, Anxiety and Phobias; from the Royal College of Psychiatrists; free, with sae.

Common illnesses

Many organisations (eg the British Heart Foundation and the Stroke Association) produce a range of publications that are either free or very reasonably priced. To find what you need, it is probably best to approach the appropriate organisation and ask for their publications list.

Family Doctor booklets cover a number of topics accurately and clearly; they are available cheaply at most chemist shops/pharmacies.

The older carer

Teach Yourself Caring for Someone at Home (1996) by Gail Elkington and Jill Harrison, published by Carers National Association, London

The Carer's Handbook: What to do and who to turn to (1993) by Marina Lewycka, published by Age Concern Books, London. There are a number of other titles in the Carers Handbook series; ask for a publications list.

In Control: Help with incontinence (1990) by Penny Mares, published by Age Concern Books, London

The Law and Vulnerable Older People (1986) edited by Sally Greengross, published by Age Concern Books, London

Dementia and Mental Illness in Older People (2nd edition 1993) by Elaine Murphy, published by Papermac/Macmillan, London and Basingstoke

I Don't Know What to Say: How to help and support someone who is dying (1988) by Dr Rob Buckman, published by Papermac/Macmillan, London and Basingstoke

Information factsheets

Age Concern England produce over 40 factsheets on a variety of subjects; those that might be of special interest to readers of this book include:

Factsheet 18 *A brief guide to money benefits;*
Factsheet 42 *Disability equipment and how to get it;*
Factsheet 5 *Dental care in retirement;*
Factsheet 23 *Help with incontinence.*

See page 149 for details about obtaining Age Concern factsheets

Alzheimer's Society publications include:

Caring for the Person with Dementia; Advice Sheets and *Information Sheets;* write to the Society for their publications list.

Useful Addresses

Action on Elder Abuse

1268 London Road
London SW16 4ER
Tel: 020 8764 7648
Elder Abuse Response Line:0808 808 8141 (Mon–Fri 10am–4.30pm)
Fax: 020 8679 4074

Information and support to anyone concerned about abuse of an older person.

Age Concern England

see page 145

Alcohol Concern

Waterbridge House
Loman Street
London SE1 0EE
Tel: 020 7928 7377
Fax: 020 7928 4644

For advice and help if you or someone you know has a drink problem refer to Drinkline,
0800 917 8282.

Alzheimer's Society

Gordon House
10 Greencoat Place
London SW1P 1PH
Tel: 020 7306 0606
Helpline: 0845 300 0336
Fax: 020 7306 0808

Advice and information to carers and families of people with dementia. There are over 300
groups and contacts in England, Wales and Northern Ireland.

Alzheimer Scotland – Action on Dementia

22 Drumsheugh Gardens
Edinburgh EH3 7RN
Tel: 0131 243 1453
Helpline: 0808 808 3000 (24 hours)
Fax: 0131 243 1450

Advice and information in Scotland to carers and families of people with dementia.

Arthritis Care

18 Stephenson Way
London NW1 2HD
Tel: 020 7916 1500
Freephone helpline: 0808 800 4050 (Monday–Friday 12–4pm)
Fax: 020 7380 6505

Information, counselling, training, fun and social contact. The first port of call for anyone with arthritis. There are many smaller organisations for particular types of arthritis. Arthritis Care's helpline can provide details.

ASH – Action on Smoking and Health

102 Clifton Street
London EC2A 4HW
Tel: 020 7739 5902

Medical charity that campaigns to alert the public on the dangers of smoking. Publishes a range of ASH factsheets. Has local groups throughout England.

Breast Cancer Care

Kiln House
210 New Kings Road
London SW6 4NZ
Tel: 020 7384 2984 (Admin)
        0808 800 6000 (Helpline: Mon–Fri 10am–5pm; Sat 10–2pm)
        0808 800 6001 (Helpline textphone)
Fax: 020 7384 3387

Information and support for people affected by breast cancer

British Association for Counselling and Psychotherapy

1 Regent Place
Rugby
Warwickshire CV21 2PJ
Tel: 01788 550 899
Fax: 01788 562 189

To find out about counselling services in your area.

British Association for Sexual and Marital Therapy

PO Box 13686
London SW20 9ZH

For help with sexual difficulties.

British Chiropractic Association

Blagrave House
17 Blagrave Street
Reading
Berks RG1 1QB
Tel: 0118 950 5950
Fax: 0118 958 8946

Professional association of practitioners of chiropractic.

British Colostomy Association

15 Station Road
Reading
Berks RG1 1LG
Tel: 0118 939 1537

For help and advice on coping with a colostomy.

British Heart Foundation

14 Fitzhardinge Street
London W1H 6DH
Tel: 020 7935 0185
      0870 600 6566 (for publications)
Fax: 020 7486 5820

Publishes the 'Heart Information' series – a range of booklets on all problems and treatments relating to heart disease.

British Lung Foundation

78 Hatton Garden
London EC1N 8LD
Tel: 020 7831 5831
Fax: 020 7831 5832

Information leaflets about all aspects of lung disease.

British Tinnitus Association

4th floor, White House Building
Fitzalan Square
Sheffield S1 2AZ
Tel: 0114 279 6600
Freephone: 0800 018 0527
Fax: 0114 279 6222

Provides information, funds research and runs self-help groups.

Cancer BACUP (British Association of Cancer United Patients)

3 Bath Place
Rivington Street
London EC2A 3JR
Tel: 020 7696 9003 (Admin)
      020 7613 2121 (Information)
      0808 800 1234 (Freephone information)
Fax: 020 7696 9002

Information and support group for people with cancer.

Cancerlink

11–21 Northdown Street
London N1 9BN
Tel: 020 7833 2818 (Admin)
Support Link: 0808 808 0000 (Mon, WEd, Fri 10am–6pm)
Fax: 020 7833 4963

Help and support for people with cancer.

Carers National Association

20–25 Glasshouse Yard
London EC1A 4JT
Tel: 020 7490 8818
Helpline: 0808 808 7777 (Mon–Fri 10am–noon; 2–4pm)
Fax: 020 7490 8824

Advice and support for carers. It campaigns for services, enables carers to speak out and provides a network of carers' support groups.

Continence Foundation

307 Hatton Square
16 Baldwins Gardens
London EC1N 7RJ
Tel: 020 7404 6875
Helpline: 020 7831 9831 (Mon–Fri 9.30am–4.30pm; staffed by continence specialist nurses)
Fax: 020 7404 6876

Information about incontinence and ways of coping with it.

Crossroads Association

(Crossroads Association Caring for Carers Scheme Ltd)
10 Regent Place
Rugby, Warwickshire CV21 2PN
Tel: England: 01788 573 653
      Wales: 029 2022 2282
      Scotland: 0141 226 3793
      Northern Ireland: 028 9181 4455

Trained care workers provide respite care for someone with care needs at home.

CRUSE – Bereavement Care

126 Sheen Road
Richmond
Surrey TW9 1UR
Tel: 020 8940 4818
Helpline: 0870 167 1677
Fax: 020 8940 7638

Bereavement advice and support. Local branches give practical advice and provide individual and group counselling as well as opportunities for social contact.

Diabetes UK

10 Queen Anne Street
London W1G 9LH
Tel: 020 7323 1531
      020 7636 6112 (Care Line)
      0800 585 088   (orderline for publications)
Fax: 020 7637 3644

For advice and support in coping with diabetes.

Disabled Living Centres Council

Redbank House
4 St Chad's Street
Manchester M8 8QA
Tel: 0161 834 1044
Fax: 0161 839 0802

For a Centre near you, where you can see aids and equipment.

Exercise England

Solecast House
13–27 Brunswick Place
London N1 6DX

Send sae for advice leaflets, and for the name of the regional representative who can supply names of qualified teachers in your area.

Extend (Exercise Training for the Elderly and Disabled)

22 Maltings Drive
Wheathampstead, Herts AL4 8QJ
Tel/Fax: 01582 832 760

Recreational movement to music for men and women over 60 and for less able people of any age.

General Chiropractic Council

344–354 Gray's Inn Road
London WC1X 8BT
Tel: 020 7713 5155

The statutory body regulating practitioners of chiropractic.

Hearing Concern

7–11 Armstrong Road
London W3 7JL
Tel: 020 8743 1110 (Admin)
Textphone: 020 8742 9151
Helpline: 0845 074 4600 (voice and textphone)
Fax: 020 8742 9043

For information and advice for people with hearing impairment.

Holiday Care

2nd floor, Imperial Buildings
Victoria Road
Horley, Surrey RH6 7PZ
Tel: 01293 774535

Information and advice about holidays for older or disabled people and those disadvantaged by low income.

Hospice Information Service

St Christopher's Hospice
51 Lawrie Park Road
London SE26 6DZ
Tel: 020 8778 9252
Fax: 020 8776 9345

Send 1st class sae for information about hospice care.

Impotence Association

PO Box 10296
London SW17 9WH
Helpline: 020 8767 7791
Fax: 020 8516 7725

For information and advice on treatment for and coping with sexual difficulties.

Lesbian and Gay Bereavement Project

Vaughan M Williams Centre
Colindale Hospital
London NW9 5HG
Tel: 020 8200 0511
Helpline: 020 8455 8894

Advice and support for homosexual people on the death of a partner.

Macmillan Cancer Relief

89 Albert Embankment
London SE1 7UQ
Tel: 020 7840 7840
Information Line: 0845 601 6161 (Mon–Fri 9.30am–7.30pm)
Fax: 020 7840 7841

Provides help and support for people with cancer through the work of Macmillan nurses.

Marie Curie Cancer Care

89 Albert Embankment
London SE1 7TP
Tel: 020 7599 7777
Fax: 020 7599 7788

Provides help, support and respite care for carers of people with cancer.

National Association of Bereavement Services

2nd floor
4 Pinchin Street
London E1 1SA
Tel: 020 7709 9090 (Referrals)
    020 7709 0505 (Admin)

Support and training for organisations working with bereaved people. Can also direct bereaved people themselves to an appropriate source of help.

National Association of Councils for Voluntary Service

3rd floor
Arundel Court
177 Arundel Street
Sheffield S1 2NU
Tel:0114 278 6636

Can tell you how to find your nearest Council, which puts volunteers in touch with people needing help.

National Asthma Campaign

Providence House
Providence Place
London N1 0NT
Tel: 020 7226 2260
Helpline: 0845 01 02 03
Fax: 020 7704 0740

Advice and booklets on asthma. Its helpline is staffed by a team of specialist asthma nurses.

National Council for Voluntary Organisations (NCVO)

Regents Wharf
8 All Saints Street
London N1 9RL
Tel: 020 7713 6161

Information about voluntary organisations in your locality that could be a source of help.

Open University

PO Box 72
Milton Keynes MK7 6AQ
Tel: 01908 653 454

For a wide range of short-term and long-term courses.

Parkinson's Disease Society

215 Vauxhall Bridge Road
London SW1V 1EJ
Tel: 020 7931 8080
Helpline: 0808 800 0303 (Mon–Fri 9.30am–5.30pm)
Fax: 020 7233 9908

Welfare support and advice, information and funds for research.

Pre-Retirement Association

9 Chesham Road
Guildford, Surrey GU1 3LS
Tel: 01483 301 170

For guidance on preparing for and enjoying retirement.

Public Trust Office

Customer Service Unit (Mental Health)
Protection Division, Stewart House
24 Kingsway, London WC2B 6JX
Tel: 020 7664 7300
Fax: 020 7664 7168

Advice about powers of attorney and handling the financial affairs of people with mental disorder.

Quitline (**Smokeline** in Scotland)

Victory House
170 Tottenham Court Road
London W1P 0HA
Tel: England: 0800 00 22 00
　　　Northern Ireland: 028 9066 3281
　　　Scotland: 0800 84 84 84
　　　Wales: 0345 697 500

For information and help with trying to stop smoking.

RADAR (Royal Association for Disability and Rehabilitation)

12 City Forum
250 City Road
London EC1V 8AF
Tel: 020 7250 3222
Textphone: 020 7250 4119
Fax: 020 7250 0212

Information and publications about aids and mobility, holidays and leisure.

Northern Ireland:
Disability Action
189 Portside Bus Park
Airport Road West
Belfast BT3 9ED
Tel: 028 9029 7880
Fax: 028 9029 7881

Scotland:
Disability Scotland
Princes House
5 Shandwick Place
Edinburgh EH2 4RG
Tel: 0131 229 8632

Wales:
Disability Wales
Wenddu Court
Caerphilly Bus Park, Van Road
Caerphilly CF83 3ED
Tel: 029 2088 8702

REACH

89 Albert Embankment
London SE1 7TP
Tel: 020 7582 6543
Fax: 020 7582 2423

Finds part-time, expenses-only jobs for retired people who want to give charities the benefit of their business and professional experience.

Relate

Herbert Gray College
Little Church Street
Rugby, Warwickshire CV21 3AP
Tel: 01788 573241

Counselling and help with difficult relationships; many local branches.

RoSPA (Royal Society for the Prevention of Accidents)

Edgbaston Park
353 Bristol Road
Birmingham B5 7ST
Tel: 0121 248 2000

Advice and publications about preventing accidents.

Royal British Legion

48 Pall Mall
London SW1Y 5JY
Tel: 020 7973 7200
Information Line: 08457 725 725
Fax: 020 7973 7399

Helps the many older people who served in the forces.

Royal College of Psychiatrists

17 Belgrave Square
London SW1X 8PG
Tel: 020 7235 2351
Fax: 020 7245 1231

For 'Help is at Hand' leaflets – on a range of subjects, including bereavement, depression, anxiety and phobias.

Royal National Institute for the Blind (RNIB)

224 Great Portland Street
London W1W 5AA
Tel: 020 7388 1266
Helpline: 08457 66 99 99
Fax: 020 7388 8316

Information about equipment and services that might help people with sight problems.

Royal National Institute for Deaf People (RNID)

19–23 Featherstone Street
London EC1Y 8SL
Tel: 020 7296 8000
Textphone Helpline: 0808 808 9000
Tinnitus Helpline: 0808 808 6666
Voice Helpline: 0808 808 0123
Helpline fax: 020 7296 8199

Information about equipment and services that might help people with hearing problems.

Society of Shoe Fitters

The Anchorage
28 Admirals walk
Hingham, Norfolk NR9 4JL
Tel/Fax: 01953 851171

Send sae plus £3 for booklet listing qualified shoe fitters who cater for particular problems (eg large, wide or narrow feet).

SPOD (Sexual and Personal Relationships of People with a Disability)

286 Camden Road
London N7 0BJ
Tel: 020 7607 8851 (Mon–Thurs 10am–4pm)
Helpline: 020 7607 9191
Fax: 020 7700 0236

Telephone counselling Monday and Wednesday 1.30–4.30pm and Tuesday and Thursday 10.30am–1.30pm.

SSAFA Forces Help

19 Queen Elizabeth Street
London SE1 2LP
Tel: 020 7403 8783
Fax: 020 7403 8815

Helps people who served (or are serving) in the forces.

Stroke Association

Stroke House
123–127 Whitecross Street
London EC1Y 8JJ
Tel: 020 7566 0300
Helpline: 0845 303 3100
Fax: 020 7490 2686

Information and advice about chest, heart and stroke illnesses. Local support groups for people who have had a stroke and their families.

UK Home Care Association

42b Banstead Road
Carshalton Beeches
Surrey SM5 3NW
Tel: 020 8288 1551
Fax: 020 8288 1550

For information about organisations providing home care in your area.

University of the Third Age (U3A)

Third Age Trust
26 Harrison Street
London WC1H 8JG
Tel: 020 7837 8838
Fax: 020 7837 8845

A network of local groups of older people who learn together in self-help groups by pooling their knowledge and experience.

About Age Concern

Better Health in Retirement is one of a wide range of publications produced by Age Concern England, the National Council on Ageing. Age Concern works on behalf of all older people and believes that later life should be fulfilling and enjoyable. For too many this is impossible. As the leading charitable movement in the UK concerned with ageing and older people, Age Concern finds effective ways to change that situation.

Where possible, we enable older people to solve problems themselves, providing as much or as little support as they need. A network of local Age Concerns, supported by 250,000 volunteers, provides community-based services such as lunch clubs, day centres and home visiting.

Nationally, we take a lead role in campaigning, parliamentary work, policy analysis, research, specialist information and advice provision, and publishing. Innovative programmes promote healthier lifestyles and provide older people with opportunities to give the experience of a lifetime back to their communities.

Age Concern is dependent on donations, covenants and legacies.

Age Concern England
1268 London Road
London SW16 4ER
Tel: 020 8765 7200
Fax: 020 8765 7211

Age Concern Scotland
113 Rose Street
Edinburgh EH2 3DT
Tel: 0131 220 3345
Fax: 0131 220 2779

Age Concern Cymru
4th Floor
1 Cathedral Road
Cardiff CF1 9SD
Tel: 029 2037 1566
Fax: 029 2039 9562

Age Concern Northern Ireland
3 Lower Crescent
Belfast BT7 1NR
Tel: 028 9024 5729
Fax: 028 9023 5497

Publications from Age Concern Books

Know Your Medicines

Pat Blair

This handy guide answers many of the common questions that older people – and those who care for them – often have about the medicines they use and how they work. The text stresses safety throughout, and covers:

- what medicines actually do
- using medicines more effectively
- getting advice and asking questions
- common ailments
- taking your medicine
- medicines and your body systems

There is also information about the dosage and strength, brands, storage and disposal, and an index to help look up medicines that are prescribed or bought over the counter.

£7.99 0–86242–226–4

Caring for someone who has dementia

Jane Brotchie

Caring for someone with dementia can be physically and emotionally exhausting, and it is often difficult to think about what can be done to make the situation easier. This book shows how to cope and seek further help as well as containing detailed information on the illness itself and what to expect in the future.

£6.99 0–86242–259–0

Caring for someone who is dying

Penny Mares

Confronting the knowledge that a loved one is going to die soon is always a moment of crisis. And the pain of the news can be compounded by the need to take responsibility for the care and support given in the last months and weeks. This book attempts to help readers cope with their emotions, identify the needs that the situation creates and make the practical arrangements necessary to ensure that the passage through the period is as smooth as possible.

£6.99 0–86242–260–4

Alive and Kicking: The carers guide to exercises for older people

Julie Sobczak with Susie Dinan and Piers Simey

Activity can play a major part in helping older people to remain agile and independent. Regular exercise can optimise levels of fitness required for the daily tasks of living, encourage social contacts, improve the feeling of well-being and help prevent future health problems.

With the wealth of ideas contained in this book, health professionals, day centre managers, residential or nursing home managers, activity organisers, relatives and carers will find plenty to stimulate the imagination. Topics covered include:

- becoming an effective instructor
- motivating the exerciser
- safety issues and medical advice
- exercise warm-ups and injury prevention
- head-to-toe chair exercises

Also provided are handy tips and ideas on how to make exercise fun, stretching and relaxation techniques and using props.

£9.99 0–86242–289–2

Your Rights: A guide to money benefits for older people

Sally West

A highly acclaimed annual guide to the state benefits available to older people. It contains information on Income Support, Housing Benefit and retirement pensions, among other matters, and provides advice on how to claim.

For further information please contact Age Concern Books in Devon.

Gardening in Retirement

Bernard Salt

Gardening in Retirement is a new and refreshing approach to gardening, aimed at retired people. It is a book for the fit and active but also contains information useful for those who experience difficulties with everyday tasks. All sections of the book have been thoroughly tried and tested by the author in his organic garden in Derbyshire. The book:

- contains numerous ideas and tips on making most jobs easier
- covers both organic and conventional approaches to gardening
- contains over 300 colour photographs, taken in the author's garden.

Subjects covered include patios, lawns, borders, greenhouses, trees, fruit and vegetables. Safety, recycling, care of wildlife and the environment are also emphasised. Highly practical, the book has something to offer everyone – from those who want to spend happy hours pursuing gardening as a hobby to others who want an easy-to-maintain yet attractive garden.

£12.99 0–86242–311–2

If you would like to order any of these titles, please write to the address below, enclosing a cheque or money order for the appropriate amount (plus £1.95 p&p) made payable to Age Concern England. Credit card orders may be made on 0870 44 22 044 (individuals) or 0870 44 22 120 (AC federation, other organisations and institutions), or fax 01626 32 33 18.

Age Concern Books
PO Box 232
Newton Abbot
Devon TQ12 4XQ

Age Concern Information Line/Factsheets Subscription

Age Concern produces 44 comprehensive factsheets designed to answer many of the questions older people (or those advising them) may have. These include money and benefits, health, community care, leisure and education, and housing. For up to five free factsheets, telephone 0800 00 99 66 (7am–7pm, seven days a week, every day of the year). Alternatively, you may prefer to write to Age Concern, FREEPOST (SWB 30375), ASHBURTON, Devon TQ13 7ZZ.

For professionals working with older people, the factsheets are available on an annual subscription service, which includes updates throughout the year. For further details and costs of the subscription, please write to Age Concern at the above Freepost address.

Index